SEE and BE

RACHEL CARR, a teacher of education and creative body development, is the author of fifteen books, including several for children.

EDWARD KIMBALL'S photographs have appeared in international magazines and books authored by his wife, Rachel Carr.

SEE and BE
yoga and creative movement for children

Rachel Carr
Photography and verses
by Edward Kimball

PRENTICE-HALL, INC., Englewood Cliffs, New Jersey 07632   A SPECTRUM BOOK

Library of Congress Cataloging in Publication Data

Carr, Rachel E
  See and be.

  (A Spectrum Book)
  SUMMARY: Gives suggestions for exercises and games for use with three- to five-year-olds to stimulate creative body movement and develop self-awareness.
  1. Yoga, Hatha—Juvenile literature. 2. Exercise—Juvenile literature. 3. Yoga, Hatha, for children. 4. Exercise for children. 1. Exercise. 2. Motor learning. 3. Yoga. I. Kimball, Edward N. II. Title.
RA781.7.C367 1980   613.7   79-23808
ISBN 0-13-799114-2
ISBN 0-13-799106-1 pbk.

© 1980 by Rachel Carr

All rights reserved. No part of this book
may be reproduced in any form
or by any means without permission in writing
from the publisher.

A SPECTRUM BOOK

10 9 8 7 6 5 4 3 2 1

Printed in the United States of America

Editorial/production supervision
by Norma Miller Karlin
Interior design by Dawn L. Stanley
Graphics by Rachel Carr
Page layout by Christine Gehring Wolf
Cover design by Dawn L. Stanley
Manufacturing buyer: Cathie Lenard

PRENTICE-HALL INTERNATIONAL, INC., *London*
PRENTICE-HALL OF AUSTRALIA PTY. LIMITED, *Sydney*
PRENTICE-HALL OF CANADA, LTD., *Toronto*
PRENTICE-HALL OF INDIA PRIVATE LIMITED, *New Delhi*
PRENTICE-HALL OF JAPAN, INC., *Tokyo*
PRENTICE-HALL OF SOUTHEAST ASIA PTE. LTD., *Singapore*
WHITEHALL BOOKS LIMITED, *Wellington, New Zealand*

CONTENTS

PREFACE FOR
    PARENTS AND TEACHERS   ix

CREDITS   xiii

HOW TO USE THIS BOOK   1

LIMBERING AND STRENGTHENING
    EXERCISES   10

EXPRESSIVE BODY SHAPES   22

RHYTHMIC MOVEMENTS FOR
    AGILITY, BALANCE,
    AND CONTROL   42

FUN WITH A PARTNER   61

GAMES CHILDREN LIKE
    TO PLAY   67

THE WORLD OF IMAGERY   70

ASSESSMENT OF PROGRESS
    CHARTS   108

PREFACE FOR PARENTS AND TEACHERS

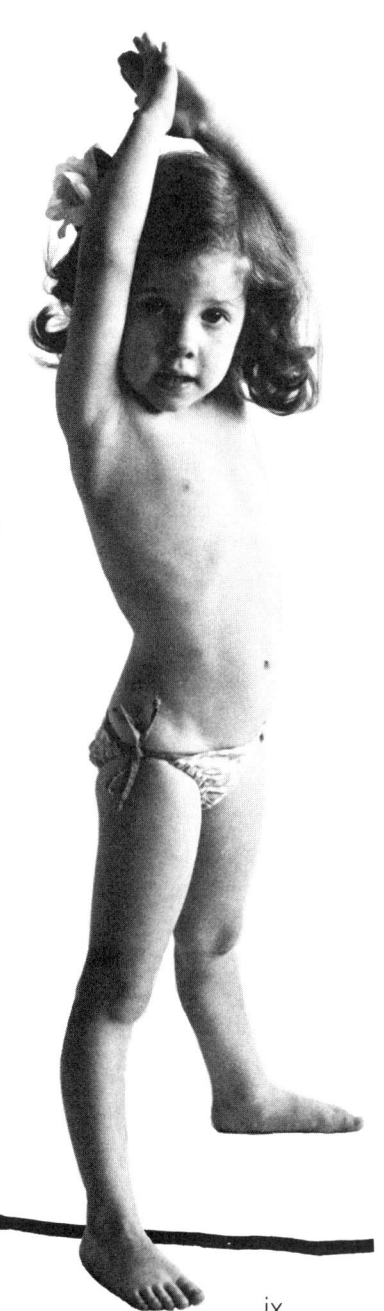

Children live in a sensory world. From the moment of birth, they need to be held and loved. Tactile stimulation, even in the animal world, is vital for normal growth. To touch, to smell, to hold, to see, to taste, to hear—these are instinctive perceptions that should be nurtured during early development. Deprived children suffer greatly from lack of human touch. In nurseries for unwanted babies "surrogate mothers" are provided to hold and love them, and to stimulate their sensory perceptions. Psychiatrists agree that a cold or neglectful parent is more dangerous to a child than an overprotective one.

During my years of experience in teaching hundreds of children creative body development, I have become aware that many of them have absolutely no sense of themselves. This generally comes from a gap created when the parent feels that the growing child no longer needs to be held and openly loved. Whatever curiosity the child may have in a desire to reach out and touch or smell something new, words of admonition—"Don't touch!—are heard rather than words that will encourage the child to explore the world.

Children should be stimulated to feel joy in movement and to be made aware of what happens inside and outside themselves. They are happy when they can enter a world of imagery where they become one with animals, birds, insects, and objects. Such intense animation gives them freedom to move, and develops their kinesthetic awareness, at the same time the key muscles are being used. This kind of early mobility inspires confidence and increases awareness of visual, spatial and tactile impressions in a child's environment.

Young children love to become involved in animation and instinctively combine sound with movement. A four-year-old who turned himself into a cobra was convincing to the other children as he slithered on the floor, raising his head and hissing.

"I am Henry the cobra!" he called out in a changed, low voice. "Watch out . . . I am crawling to look for food. Hiss! Hiss! Hiss! Here I come . . . "

These ominous sounds were heard in the silent room, and the children gave way to Henry as he slithered in snakelike action.

The body shapes in this book challenge creative impulses, and make children take a closer look at the images, identifying them with their own bodies. They learn to move within limited space, using their own force and imagination. They learn control and balance by holding a shape, then changing directions and moving in different planes. They learn to listen and to think while moving, reacting quickly to directions of right and left, up and down, front and back. When they become sufficiently stimulated and self-directed, they begin to explore a heightened sense of themselves. Every form of creative movement they are able to do expands and deepens their instinctive capacity for rhythm. If properly channeled, creative movement enables children to use their bodies as musical instruments.

I have used this vehicle of creative body development with the handicapped. They were fascinated by the different body shapes they were able to imitate. Handicapped children have a way of communicating simply and directly with one another, inspiring confidence with a language they have in common. They seem to understand each other's needs and readily offer help. Bobby, a five-year old with cerebral palsy, wanted desperately to become a stork. It required a degree of muscular control to maintain the balance on one leg. He struggled valiantly with this image but kept losing his balance. A deaf-mute boy, perfectly coordinated, ran to Bobby's aid. In sign language he explained that if Bobby put his right side against the wall he could stand on the right foot and bend the left one back. He placed Bobby close to the wall and picked up his left leg, moving it back, then took his hands and put them in front with the palms touching. He stood back to examine the image. Not entirely satisfied, he bent Bobby's head slightly forward to suggest a stork asleep.

"Good! Good!" the children applauded.

Joy shone from Bobby's face. Timothy, the deaf-mute, was equally jubilant at his own success in helping Bobby achieve the image of the stork. He bowed to accept part of the applause.

Deaf-mutes live in a silent world and need encouragement to feel the inner rhythm of their bodies, even though they may have good motor coordination. Once the barrier is broken, they become more responsive to their own internal rhythms and move with astonishing agility and grace.

Rhythm is an intangible part of nature. Few of us are conscious of how it works in the human body. Rhythm controls the heartbeat, respiration, neuromuscular coordination. If this subtle rhythm is broken, disruption prevails and the body is thrown out of kilter.

As parents and teachers, we owe it to our children to make them aware of their own body rhythm early in life. It will stimulate their creative impulses, and such experiences are the basis from which all rhythmic learning evolves.

Motor skills are not mechanical. They should be taught rhythmically and creatively to bring out individual expression, and combined with aural and visual experiences so important to sensory development. Motor skills help to identify movement patterns with sound patterns, as a frog jumping and croaking, or a loose-limbed monkey screeching while walking.

Through development of self-awareness, children begin to discover facets of their own personalities and find their own ways of expressive movement where body and mind work in harmony.

CREDITS

The children in this book are average three- to five-year-olds learning the joy of creative movement. Much of the credit goes to their parents who have helped them become familiar with the body shapes they learned.

My husband, Edward Kimball, took the pictures in our apartment, where the children felt at home. He joked with them so they would be unaware of the camera. When they selected their favorites, he asked a three-year-old (page 24) how skinny she could be. She replied, "This much," tightening her muscles to maximum strength. A four-year-old (page 21) said, "Look at my stomach and see how fat I can be when I breathe in, and how thin I can be when I breathe out. A five-year-old (page 57), eager to show off his physical prowess, asked, "Do you want to see the best jack-in-the-box and jumping jack? . . . Watch me!" This is how the children were caught in action while totally absorbed in themselves.

We hope our book will be an inspiration to parents and teachers who devote their love and energy to the care of growing children, making them physically fit and more aware of themselves.

HOW TO USE THIS BOOK

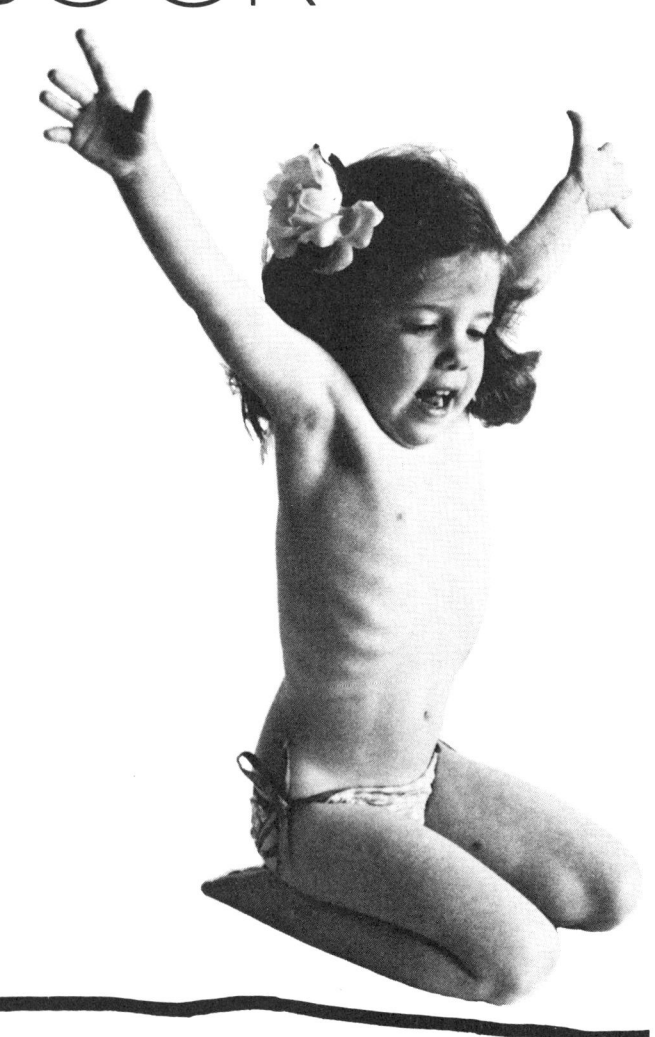

As an inspirational guide to creative body development for children ages three to five, this book can be followed step by step, or it can be used simply to provide ideas for creative movement.

There is a common belief among adults that all children are supple and can do just about anything with their bodies. This is a fallacy. Very young children have shown evidence of muscular imbalances that cause flat feet, bow-legs, knock-knees, weak ankles, stiff spine, and a host of other ailments that are frequently the result of poor muscle function. Most of these imbalances can be corrected by exercise dealing with specific groups of muscles.

An understanding of how the human body works will help to improve posture, correct muscle imbalance, and increase the range of flexibility. Think of the human body as a skeletal framework with moving parts, superbly rigged and balanced with hinges and joints. The jointed framework is made up of over 200 bones and cartilages, and some 600 muscles. The bones of children contain a greater amount of animal matter than those of adults. Children are therefore more flexible. The mineral matter which gives the bones their hardness increases with age, causing the bones to become more brittle.

The joints hold the bones together in a way that makes them capable of moving, at the same time they are held in place by ligaments or connective tissue. Some joints move freely, others move only slightly to perform the varied types of movement such as bending, straightening, moving upward, sideways, and downward. Of the freely movable joints, the ball-and-socket joints (in which the round head of one bone fits into a cuplike cavity of another) in the shoulder and hip are able to perform the varied movements. The hinge joints can only perform movements involving *flexion* (bending at a joint) or *extension* (straightening a joint).

There are three types of muscles: *voluntary, involuntary,* and *cardiac.* The voluntary muscles are controlled at will. They contract and relax like cables whose pull on bones make motion possible, such as throwing a ball, dancing, or walking. Involuntary muscles control all automatic functions, such as those involved in intestinal action. The cardiac or heart muscle is about the size of a clenched fist. Also involuntary, this special muscle operates under the influence of complex electrical signals of the nervous system.

When muscles are in normal balance the body works smoothly, but when they are thrown out of control, there is stress and strain on the joints. Muscles work in pairs. One contracts to pull a bone forward, while the other pulls it back. The muscular system is capable of an endless variety of movements. If a muscle is rigid or short, strain is felt on the joint. This strain will be eased by gentle limbering and stretching exercises to increase muscular elasticity. During exercise, muscles require more oxygen from the bloodstream.

Each body has its own skeletal structure, musculature, and center of gravity. There are loose-muscled and tight-muscled people. Movements that require bending forward with knees straight, or bending backward, must be taught cautiously to tight-muscled children, whose range of flexibility is limited. By constant limbering exercises, muscles will lengthen and tone will improve.

When children learn to be aware of their body signals, they become conscious of subtle changes that take place after stretching and limbering.

A four-year-old exclaimed excitedly, "Look! I can cross my legs, and my knees don't hurt one single bit!" Another child, calling my attention to her physical feat, shouted, "Wow! I can touch my toes to my head. Only yesterday I couldn't even do that!"

In my classes I have frequently picked out children with different skeletal structures to show how they are built. Johnny, a four-year-old, had tight knee joints but a flexible spine. Five-year-old Susan was tight-muscled with a limited flexibility range. Jamie, another five-year-old, had the ideal body, supple and well-coordinated. When I asked the class what exercises these children could do, all hands were raised.

"Johnny must do this exercise," one of the girls said, bending her left leg over the right thigh and pressing down gently on her knee, "then his knees will be OK."

Another child commented, "Susan must do all the exercises for her shoulders and her knees and her back, so her muscles can move better."

Jamie was the envy of the group, but the children were aware that she, too, must exercise to keep her muscles well-toned.

We talked about how far a muscle can stretch and how careful one must be. The children learned to stretch slowly, and the moment they felt any pain they stopped. They became so aware of their bodies that they "listened" for all kinds of signals. A three-year-old flexed his biceps, bragging to a girl his age that he was very, very strong. She touched his muscle, then put her ear close to it. "I wanna hear it," she said.

The age groups differ not only in motor coordination but in attention span as well. Three-year-olds have an attention span of about 20 minutes; four- and five-year-olds can pay attention for 30 to 40 minutes, depending on how imaginative the teacher is. If there is sufficient diversion, interest can be held beyond the general attention span.

Start each session with stretching and limbering. Make simple games out of these exercises to avoid monotony: How tall can you be? How small can you be? How skinny can you be? How wide can you be? When you are introducing a body shape of a familiar image, such as a bird, talk about it first so the image will become real. Invent games to involve children in the rhythmic movement of a bird fluttering its wings, or poised for flight, or asleep with its wings folded. Children are highly imaginative, and with little incentive can create their own images and relate to them intimately. Allow them freedom of expression.

When this concept is applied to the different body shapes, it will induce children to develop the ability to take off from a stimulus, rather than merely imitating an image to precision. *Let them be what they see.* As they begin to explore the world around them, their sensory perceptions will evoke deeper responses within themselves. They will discover that they can move in a variety of ways to explore dimensions of space, and that they can create force within their bodies by using just the right amount of muscular tension. As they become aware of what their bodies can do, they will move into other realms of physical expression.

There are children who have little sense of self-worth and need to be coaxed, held, and encouraged to gain some sense of importance.

Visual aids help to stimulate mental response; you can use pictures, drawings, or cutouts of different animals, birds, insects, and objects so the children can identify with the body shapes they learn. Visualaids should be large, and mounted so they can be seen easily for constant reference. When memorized, the images can be turned into guessing games, pantomime, contests in balance and control, and speed races.

Encourage children to help one another so they will become more aware of each other's needs. This also establishes closer rapport.

A teacher should not attempt to handle more than ten children in a group without an assistant. Individual attention is important.

There is never any danger that children can harm themselves, since no equipment is needed except area rugs or skid-proof exercise mats. Single mats are better because they become the private domain of each child. When the same mat must be shared, confusion and tears frequently occur with small children.

Freedom of movement is important. Children should be able to move easily in light stretch shorts and tops, and in their stocking feet.

With a little imagination and resourcefulness a lot can be done with the body shapes given in this book to develop creative energy and rhythmic response. Children become motivated when they are sufficiently inspired, and grow within themselves, gaining confidence and self-awareness.

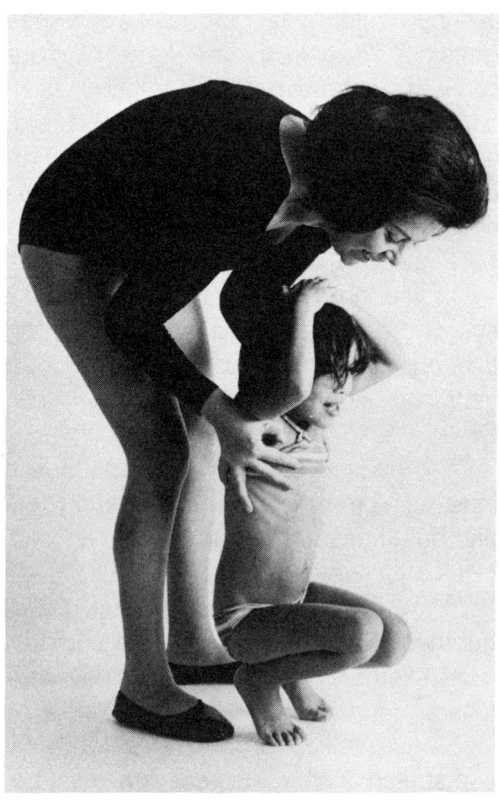

HOW TO USE THIS BOOK

Establish close rapport with children to give them confidence. Coax them, hold them, make them laugh. Let them feel your presence.

HOW TO USE THIS BOOK

When children help each other, they develop confidence, self-assurance, and the ability to form closer relationships.

HOW TO USE THIS BOOK

A five-year-old instructs a three-year-old: "When you do the woodchopper, it's this way."

HOW TO USE THIS BOOK

 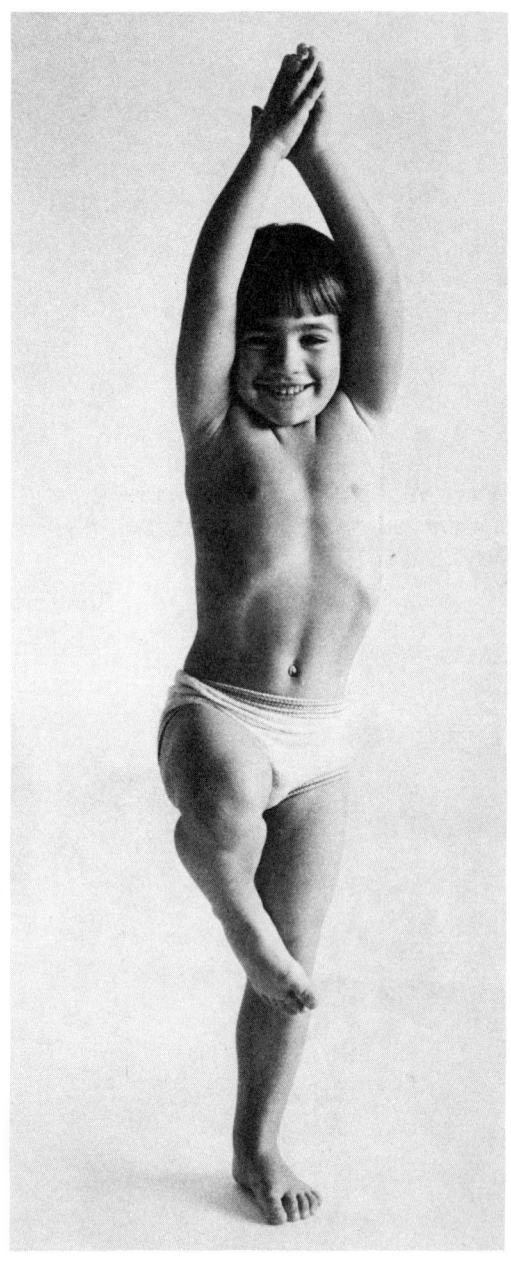

A four-year-old assists a three-year-old. "I'll hold you—then pretty soon you can stand by yourself and be a tree."

HOW TO USE THIS BOOK

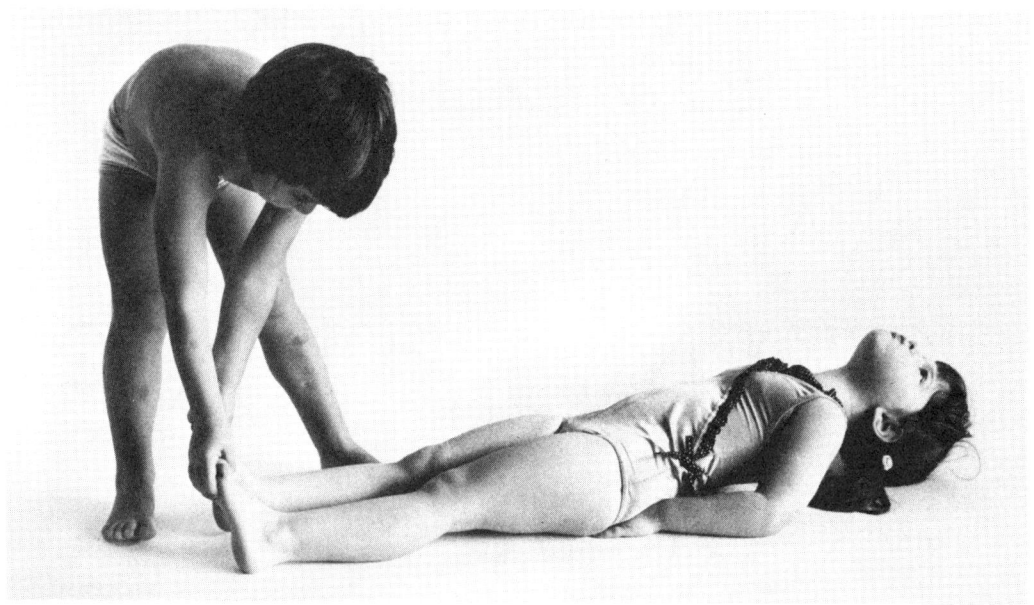

"You must keep your feet together when you are a fish," a three-year-old instructs a girl his age.

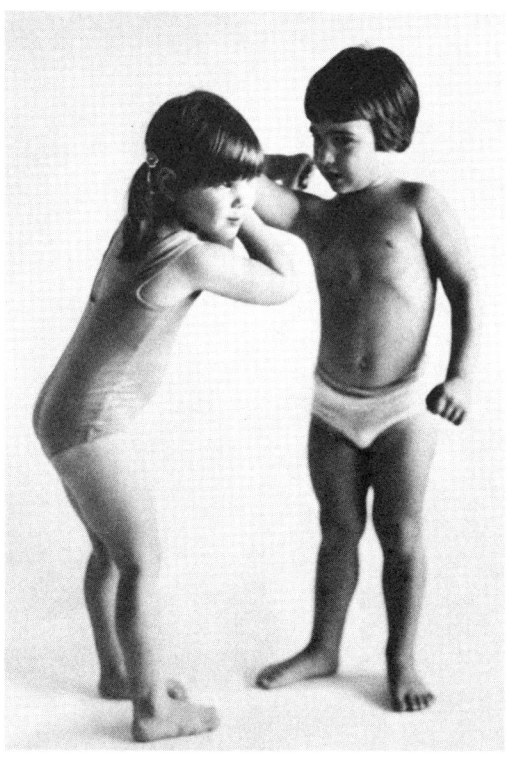

His confidence assured, he says to her, "Feel how strong my muscles are." "I wanna hear it," she responds, pressing his arm.

HOW TO USE THIS BOOK

LIMBERING AND STRENGTHENING EXERCISES

Flexibility, muscle tone, and coordination are developed by constant stretching, bending, and balancing movements. Repetition is important, and each exercise should be held for seconds at a time to develop muscular skills.

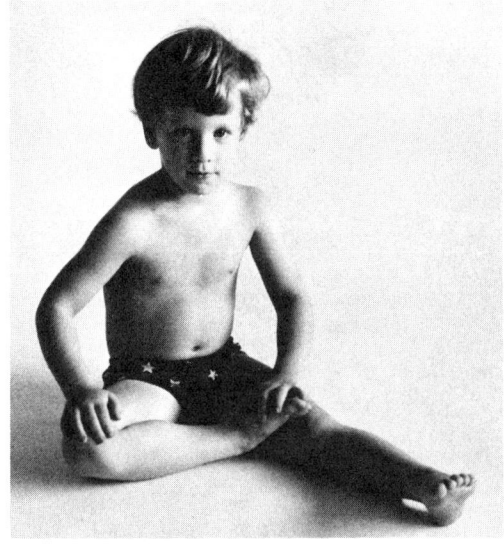

Bend right leg over left thigh and hold the foot with left hand. Press down gently on the knee with right hand. Repeat with left leg.

LIMBERING KNEES

Bring soles of feet together. Press down gently on knees with both hands.

LIMBERING AND STRENGTHENING EXERCISES

Bring soles of feet together; grasp with both hands. Pull gently toward the crotch.

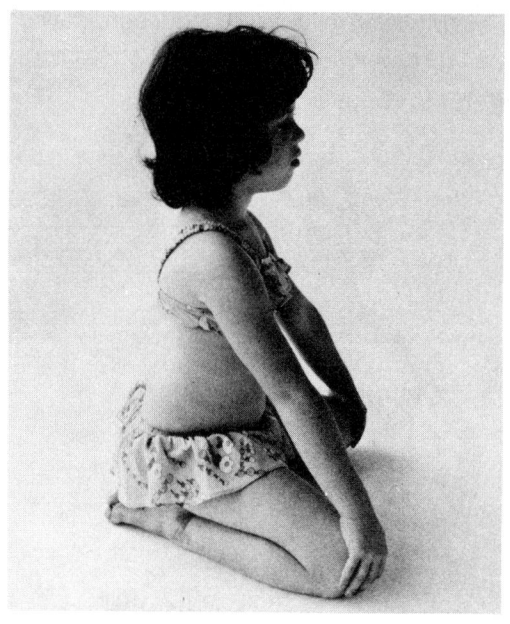

Sit on heels with legs bent back. With spine straight, rest hands on knees.

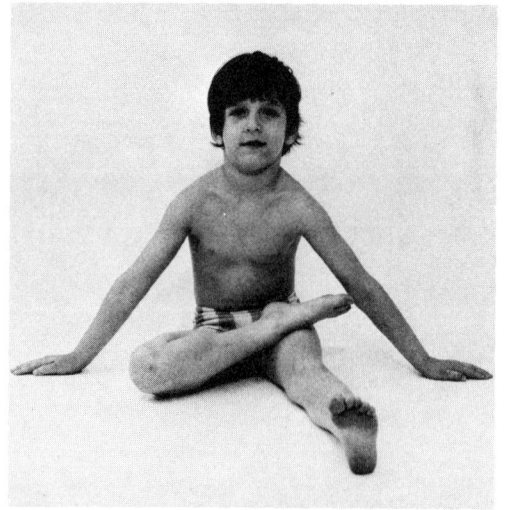

When leg muscles have increased in elasticity, place right leg over left thigh close to the crotch, then left leg over the right thigh.

Repeat with legs reversed. (Not all children are able to achieve this degree of flexibility, and should not be forced.)

LIMBERING AND STRENGTHENING EXERCISES

LOW BACK STRETCHES

Tight-muscled children should be coaxed gently into these forward stretches, which are held for seconds at a time to increase the spinal extension. Legs are spread far apart, neck is relaxed.

Bend forward to grasp left leg with both hands. Stretch far forward without straining.

LIMBERING AND STRENGTHENING EXERCISES

Place hands in front, palms down. Bend forward, sliding hands away from the body to increase spinal stretch. Hold to feel the stretch.

LIMBERING AND STRENGTHENING EXERCISES

As spinal stretch increases, let hands slide forward to touch the feet, head lowered.

LIMBERING AND STRENGTHENING EXERCISES

ROLLING MOVEMENTS TO INCREASE FLUID MOTION

ROLL FROM SIDE TO SIDE *Lie on the right side with right arm stretched under the head, and left arm over the head. Keep knees straight, legs together. Roll over on the back to the left side, then roll over to the right. Repeat several times.*

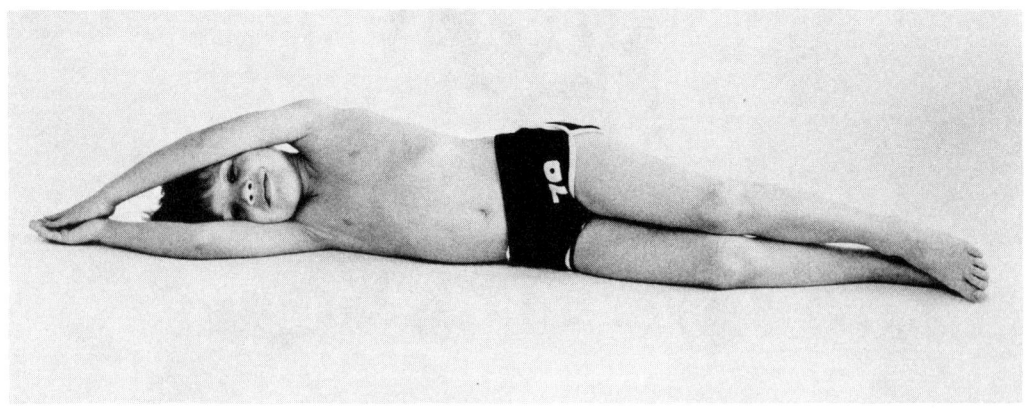

ROLL BACKWARD AND FORWARD *It takes practice for young children to be able to roll backward and forward in fluid motion with legs straight. Let them bend their knees at first to strengthen abdominal and low back muscles.*

LIMBERING AND STRENGTHENING EXERCISES

Bend forward, legs apart, head low, palms down. Press on palms; at the same time use back and abdominal muscles to swing legs over the head. Keep legs apart so feet will touch the ground, or come close.

Then press down on palms and use back and abdominal muscles to swing legs forward, keeping the head down by arching the neck.

LIMBERING AND STRENGTHENING EXERCISES

CURLING TOES TO STRENGTHEN FEET

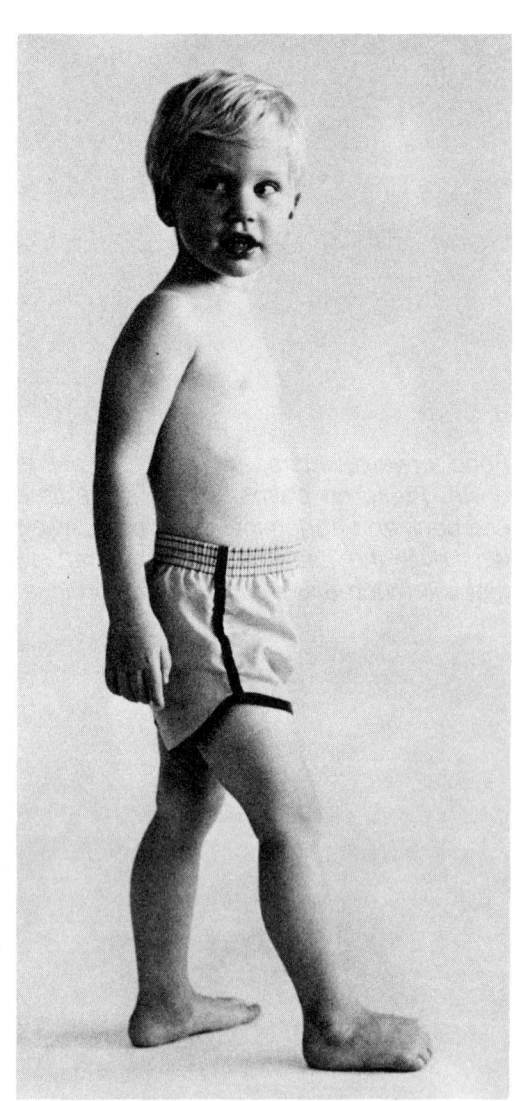

Sit with knees bent and feet close together. Curl toes, turning them inward. Hold to feel the pull. Repeat several times.

Walk slowly; with each step curl toes inward as if picking up pebbles.

BODY TWIST *Stand with legs apart, hands on waist. Bend to the right, stretching muscles. Hold, then bend to the left. Hold.*
Rotate waist in a circle: forward, right, back, and left. Reverse rotation.

BALANCE ON ONE LEG *Stand on right leg with left leg bent back. Arms are loose and away from the body to maintain balance. Hold. Repeat with left leg.*

LIMBERING AND STRENGTHENING EXERCISES

DEEP BREATHING

Breathing exercises revitalize cells of the body and brain, and flush the bloodstream with oxygen. They need not be tedious or mechanical when taught to young children.

Explain how lungs are like balloons, inflating with air, and deflating as the air goes out. The children should hear their breath. When they breathe in deeply through the nostrils, they become "fat," and when they breathe out through the mouth, they become "thin."

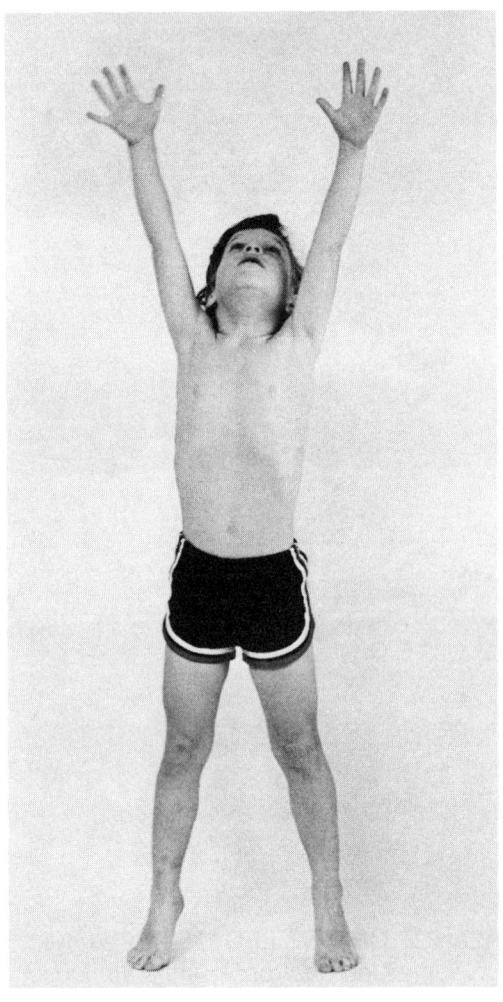

Breathe in deeply and stretch upward.

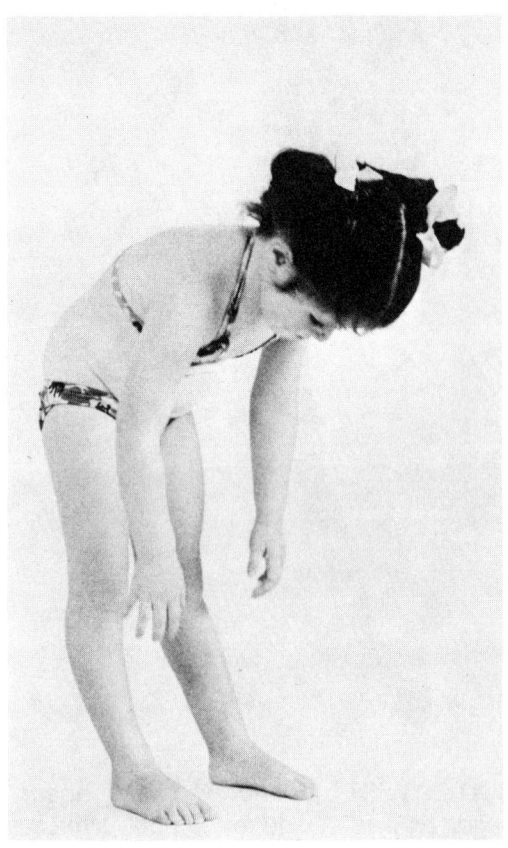

Breathe out and bend down, arms loose and knees straight.

LIMBERING AND STRENGTHENING EXERCISES

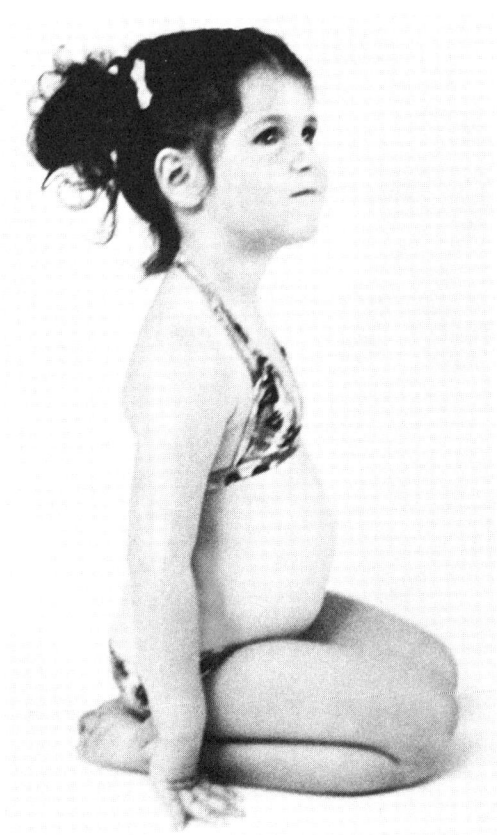

Breathe in and be fat.

Breathe out and be thin.

LIMBERING AND STRENGTHENING EXERCISES

EXPRESSIVE BODY SHAPES

Children are fascinated with the different body shapes they can become. Four- and five-year-olds have better muscular coordination and balance than three-year-olds. However, many very young children are quite capable of doing the more difficult movements and should be encouraged to try them.

The level of ability, creativity, and concentration varies in children. Some are alert and show intense absorption in listening and in doing; others are passive and lack incentive and concentration. Such lethargic children usually have a poor image of themselves, but they will brighten up and participate more enthusiastically if given a little praise and encouragement. The more familiar children become with these movements, the better they like them.

BE SMALL Bend down and touch the ground.

BE TALL Stand on tiptoe and stretch upward, reaching for the sky.

EXPRESSIVE BODY SHAPES

BE WIDE Stand with legs apart. Stretch arms to the sides. Tighten muscles to increase the stretch.

BE THIN Stand with legs together, knees pressing, and arms close to the body. Squeeze all muscles.

EXPRESSIVE BODY SHAPES

BE ROUND Sit with knees bent and arms around the legs. Tuck head between knees and arch the spine to make the body round.

BE A CAT The range of motion involves muscles of the back, arms, and legs.

SINK AND ARCH THE BACK *Get down on all fours. Sink the back in and look up, stretching the neck. Then arch the back with head down.*

EXPRESSIVE BODY SHAPES

KICK ONE LEG *While on all fours, kick the right leg straight up, pointing the toes. Turn head to look at the raised foot. Repeat with the left leg.*

STRETCH *While on all fours, stretch the entire body, keeping arms and legs straight, head down.*

EXPRESSIVE BODY SHAPES

BE A FISH Children respond to the imagery of a fish floating. They need help in arching the spine before they are able to do it by themselves. When back muscles are sufficiently strong, introduce the fin.

Lie on back with knees bent. Slip hands under lower back. Straighten legs and arch the spine. Elbows support the arch between the top of the head and lower back.

Slip hands away from the body and place them on the chest to make the fin.

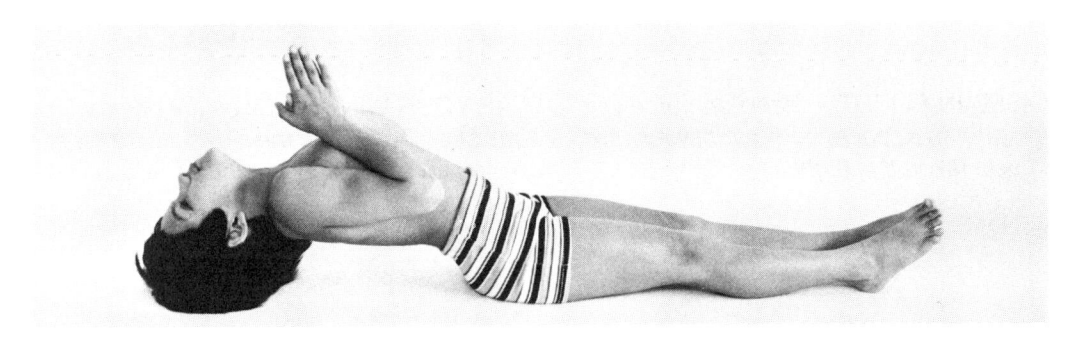

EXPRESSIVE BODY SHAPES

BE A BIRD Self-expression is important. Children can experience the sensation of being a bird flying, flapping its wings, and stretching.

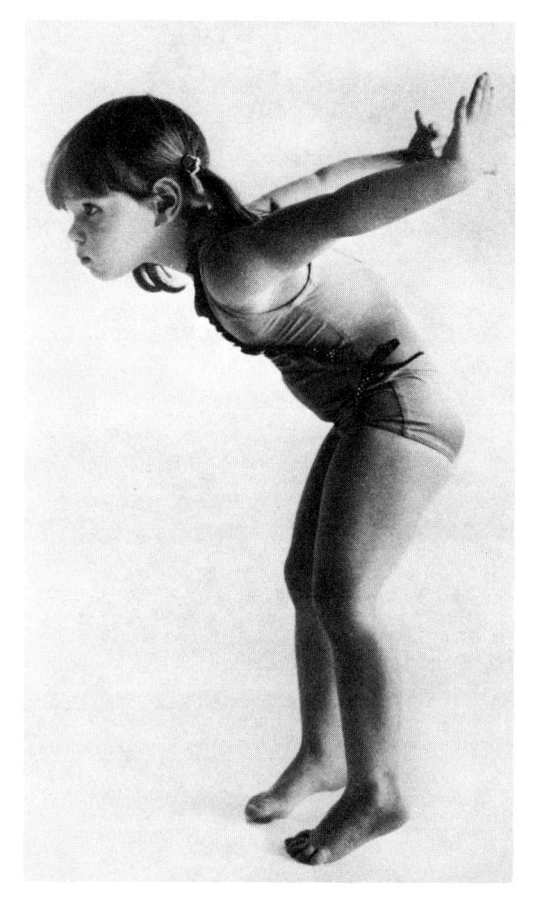

POISED IN FLIGHT *Stand on tiptoe with arms stretched back, body slightly forward, ready to take off in flight.*

FLAP YOUR WINGS *Sit on the heels with arms stretched out to the sides. Move them up and down, using muscular tension to flap the wings.*

EXPRESSIVE BODY SHAPES

STRETCH UPWARD *Sit on heels. Take a deep breath and raise arms above the head, stretching them with palms touching. Tense the body while stretching.*

STRETCH DOWNWARD *Breathe out and bend forward and down, arms outstretched, buttocks resting on the heels.*

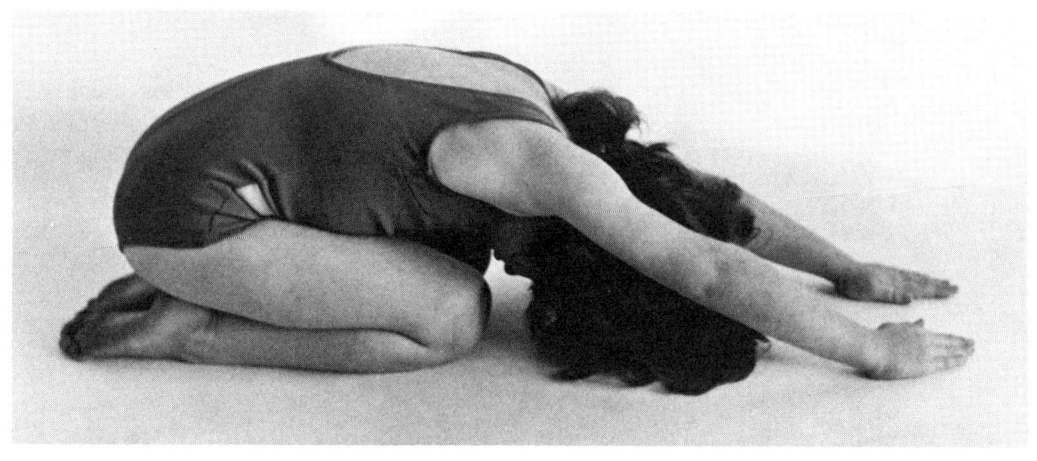

EXPRESSIVE BODY SHAPES

LETTERS OF THE ALPHABET

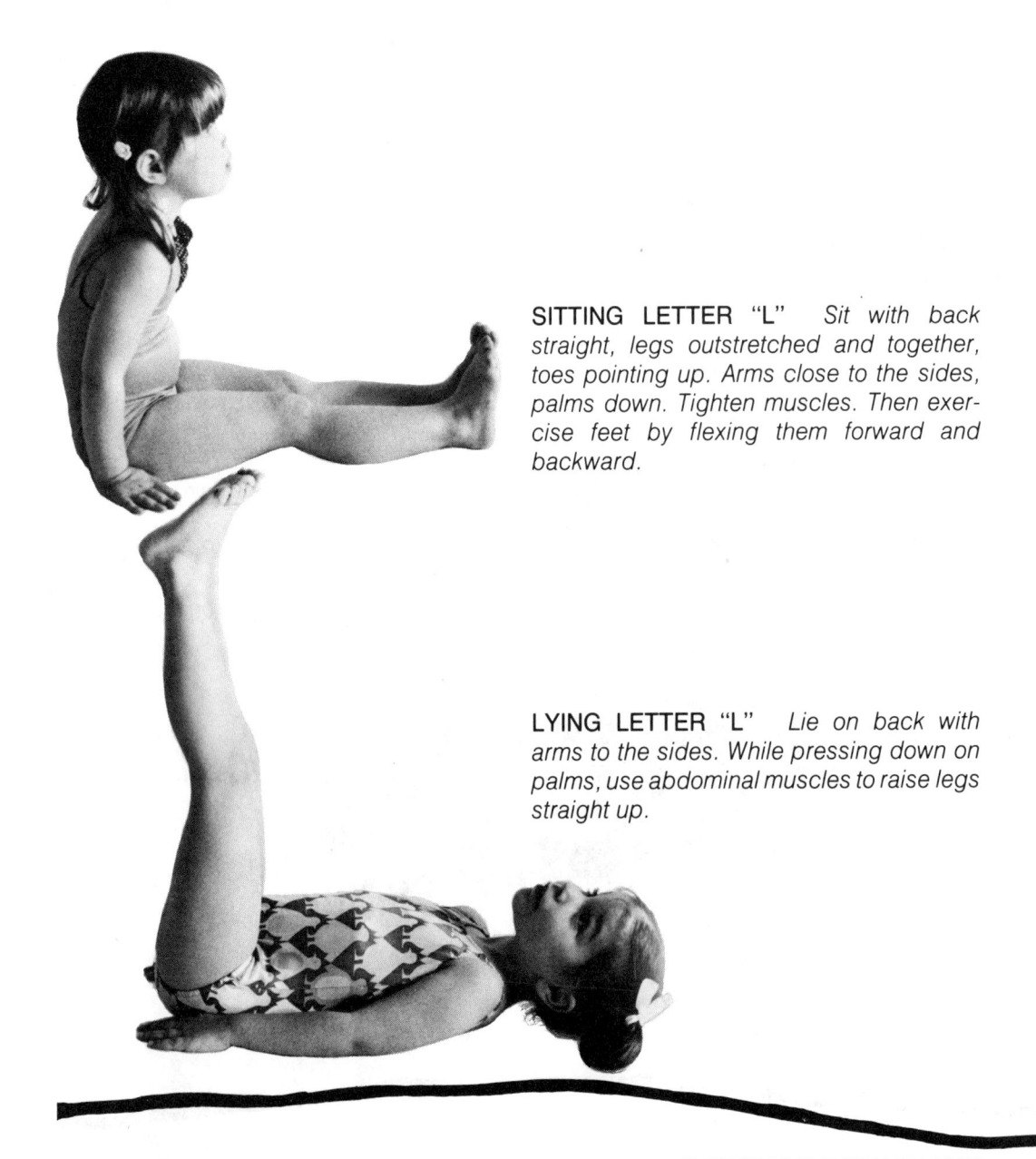

SITTING LETTER "L" Sit with back straight, legs outstretched and together, toes pointing up. Arms close to the sides, palms down. Tighten muscles. Then exercise feet by flexing them forward and backward.

LYING LETTER "L" Lie on back with arms to the sides. While pressing down on palms, use abdominal muscles to raise legs straight up.

EXPRESSIVE BODY SHAPES

CREATIVE BODY SHAPES

BE A CAMEL To give young children confidence, support the back so they can become aware of the distance between the head and feet. Once their confidence is gained, children have no trouble with this exercise, done here by a three-year-old being helped by his sister.

EXPRESSIVE BODY SHAPES

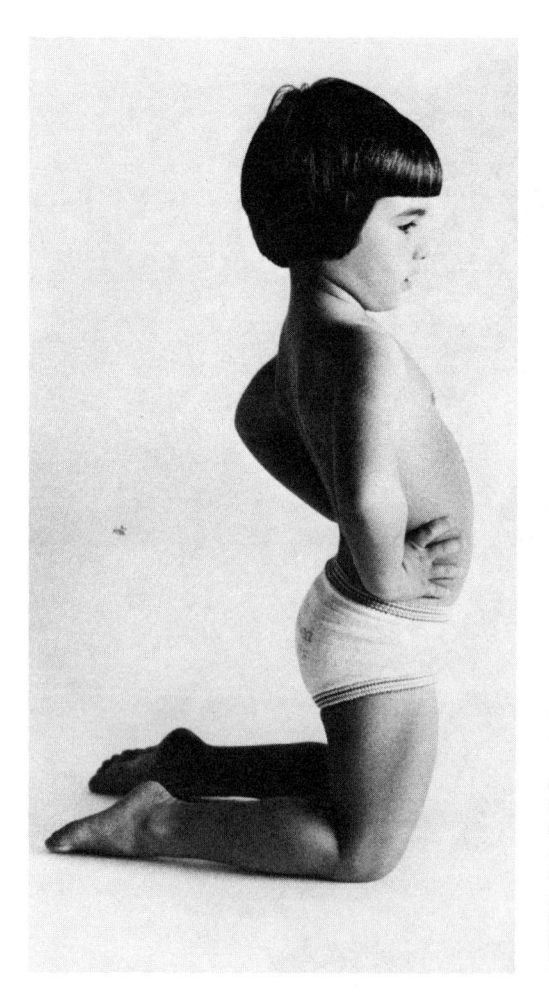

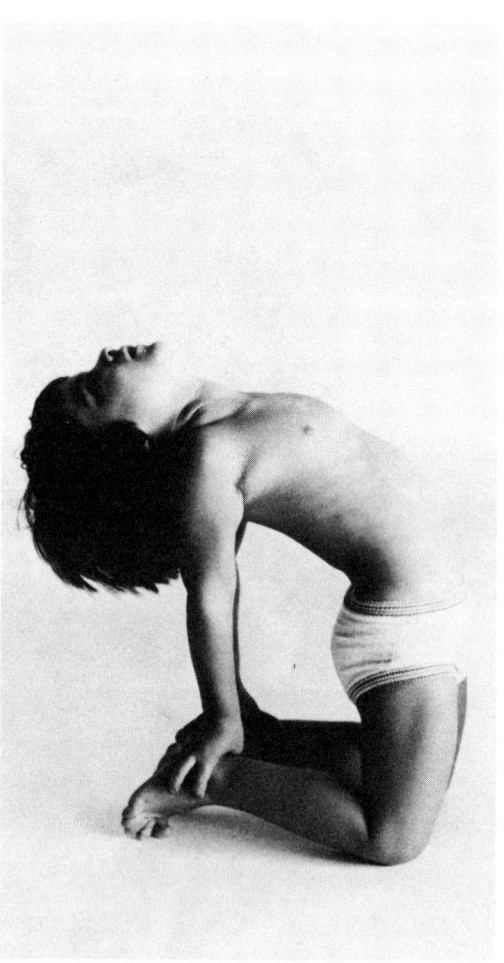

Kneel with hands on the waist, legs apart. Bend back to touch the ankles. Neck is relaxed. Hold to increase the spinal stretch.

EXPRESSIVE BODY SHAPES

BE A HARE A flexible child can do the head-to-knee stretch easily, but one who is tight-muscled needs practice to increase the spinal stretch. This exercise is excellent for bringing a fresh supply of blood to the brain.

SITTING HARE *Sit on heels. Hold onto the feet with back straight. Hold to stretch tight knees.*

SLEEPING HARE *Bend forward without letting go of the feet. Stretch arms fully. Raise the buttocks, arch the spine so head can come close to the knees. Hold to increase the spinal stretch.*

EXPRESSIVE BODY SHAPES

BE A MOUNTAIN The different body shapes of the legs, in degrees of flexibility, represent the base of a mountain. To simulate a strong and tall mountain, sit in a loose cross-legged pose. The back is straight and arms are fully stretched. Palms or fingertips touch. Reverse each movement of the legs to tone and stretch them equally.

EXPRESSIVE BODY SHAPES

Sit with one leg crossed on top of the other.

Sit with the left leg crossed high up over the right thigh, and right leg over the left thigh.

EXPRESSIVE BODY SHAPES

BE A SWAN Little bodies yield to stretching if it is done gently and gradually. This five-year-old practiced being a swan for two weeks until she was able to touch her toes to her head, but not all children can achieve this degree of flexibility, and should not be forced. They can still imagine they are swans, stretching as far as their bodies will allow.

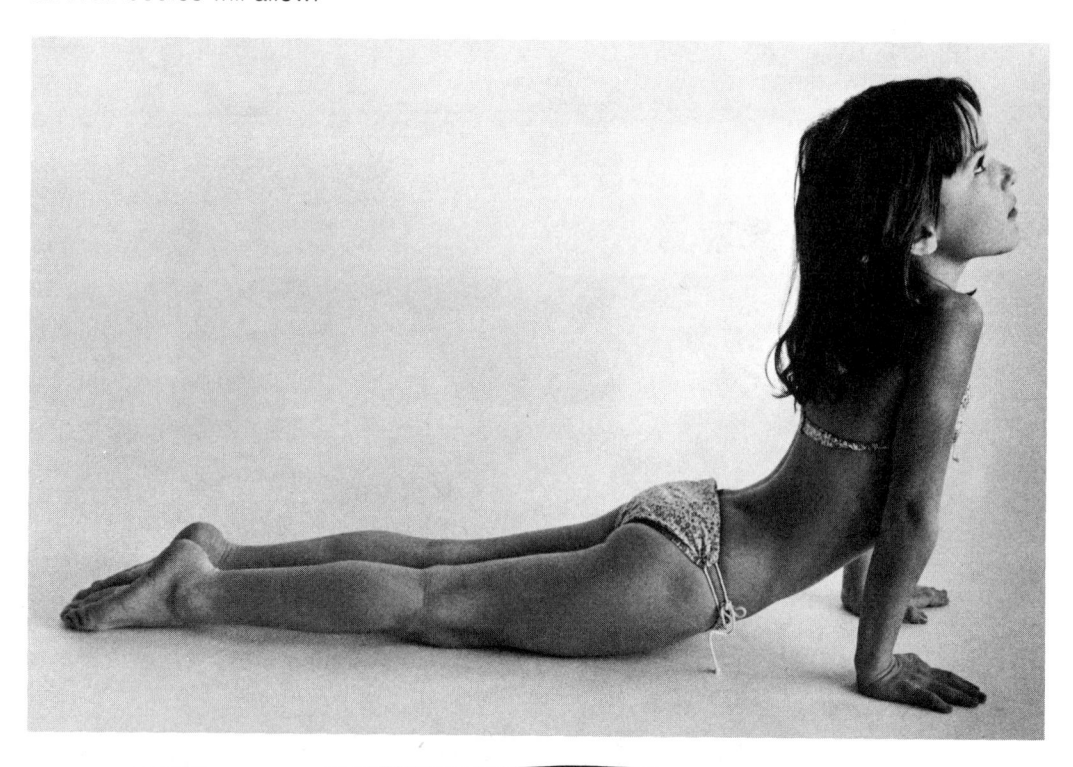

EXPRESSIVE BODY SHAPES

Lie face down, elbows bent, with palms close to the shoulders. Raise the torso first with arms fully stretched. Bend the legs up and keep them separated. Stretch daily to lengthen rigid muscles.

EXPRESSIVE BODY SHAPES

BE A STORK Concentration is the key to this balancing exercise.

Stand on the left leg, bend the right one back. Bend the head slightly forward, with palms touching, in front. (Some children form a sleeping stork by placing their hands close to the chest; others do so with their hands touching the chin.) Hold for a few seconds to steady the balance. Repeat with the other leg.

EXPRESSIVE BODY SHAPES

BE A SLIDE When the body is balanced on a plane, muscles are held taut to feel an inner force of strength.

Sit with legs outstretched and together. Palms are down, fingers point away from the body. Press on the palms and feet to raise the torso, with no sag in the middle. Keep neck relaxed with head back. Hold to increase muscular control.

EXPRESSIVE BODY SHAPES

BE A TREE Good balance is needed to hold the body against the force of gravity. A wall should be used as temporary support until balance is secure. Children can imagine themselves as a strong tree: arms are the leafy branches, body is the trunk, one leg is the root, the other is a bent branch. If they stand straight and tall, they will be like a tree that does not fall even when the wind blows. Three-year-olds are not expected to have the same muscular control as older children. This three-year-old holds his own next to the five-year-old.

Stand firmly on the right leg. Bend the left knee and rest the foot against the inner right leg. Raise arms over the head with fingertips or palms touching. Hold balance. Repeat with the other leg.

EXPRESSIVE BODY SHAPES

LETTERS OF THE ALPHABET

Maintaining balance for these body shapes involves interplay of muscles working to keep the body on its base. With constant practice, children develop better balance.

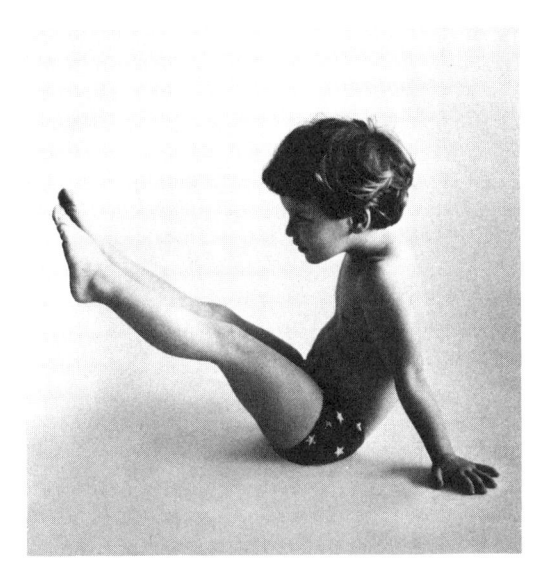

LETTER "V" Sit with legs outstretched and together, arms to the sides. Press down on the palms to lift up the legs, keeping them straight.

FLYING LETTER "V" Once balance is secure in the shape of the "V", raise arms to the sides, tensing all muscles. Four- and five-year-olds enjoy the challenge of this balancing shape.

EXPRESSIVE BODY SHAPES

RHYTHMIC MOVEMENTS FOR AGILITY, BALANCE, AND CONTROL

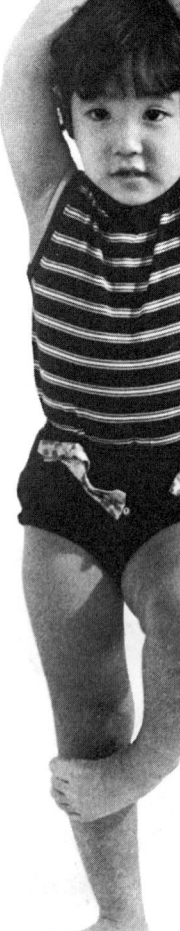

BE AN AIRPLANE Stand straight, legs together, arms stretched out. To wind up the engine, move arms up and down without bending the elbows. As plane takes off, zoom in large circles without bending the elbows.

BE A WINDMILL Stand straight with one hand on the hip, the other straight up. To get the windmill started, move the straight arm in a circle, first slowly, then increasing the speed. Repeat with the other arm. Then circle both arms.

RHYTHMIC MOVEMENTS FOR AGILITY, BALANCE, AND CONTROL

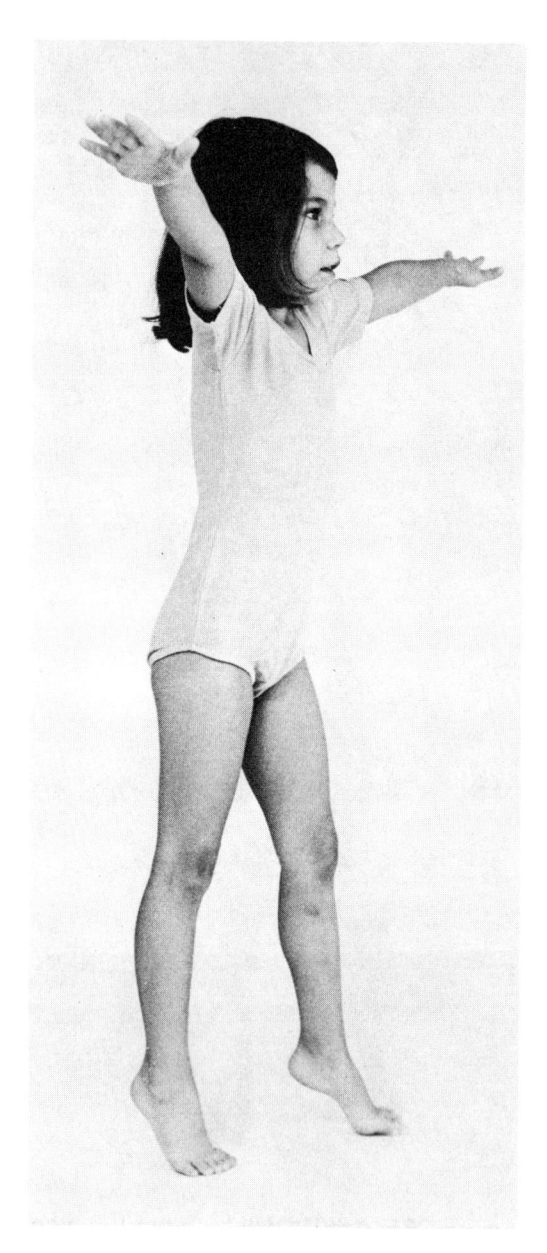

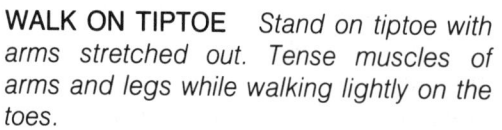

WALK ON TIPTOE *Stand on tiptoe with arms stretched out. Tense muscles of arms and legs while walking lightly on the toes.*

TIPTOE A STRAIGHT LINE *Follow a straight line with one foot crossing over the other on tiptoe.*

RHYTHMIC MOVEMENTS FOR AGILITY, BALANCE, AND CONTROL

PROWL LIKE A LION Get down on all fours and move like a loose-limbed lion.

RHYTHMIC MOVEMENTS FOR AGILITY, BALANCE, AND CONTROL 45

WALK LIKE AN ELEPHANT Get down on all fours and walk rigidly, keeping arms and legs stiff.

HOP LIKE A FROG The balancing frog involves hopping and jumping, using the right amount of force and speed that can be controlled. Lightness and agility come with practice. Some three-year-olds find it easier to hop and jump with feet securely on the ground and palms down; others are able to put their hands over their heads. Four- and five-year-olds have better muscular control and are able to hop and jump on their toes with fingers interlocked over the head.

Frog races are fun, and children never tire of them.

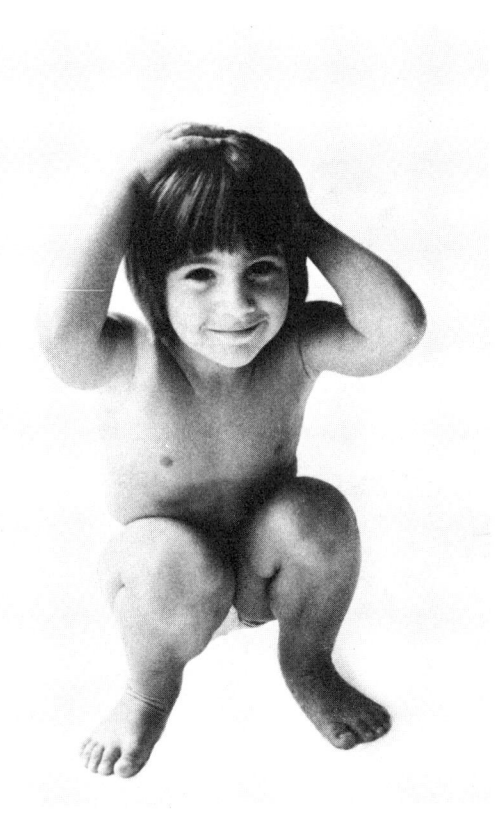

RHYTHMIC MOVEMENTS FOR AGILITY, BALANCE, AND CONTROL

MOVE LIKE A COBRA The movements of raising and lowering the spine develop agility and strength in back muscles. Neck, arms, and legs are also involved. Children will instinctively hiss and slither when imitating a cobra.

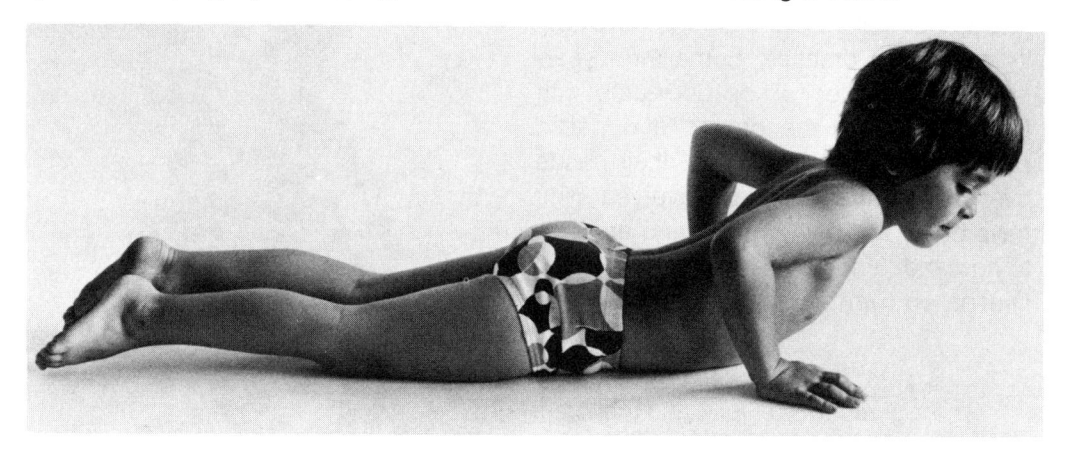

CRAWL *Lie face down arms close to the shoulders, elbows bent. Raise the head, and push body forward using hands and feet.*

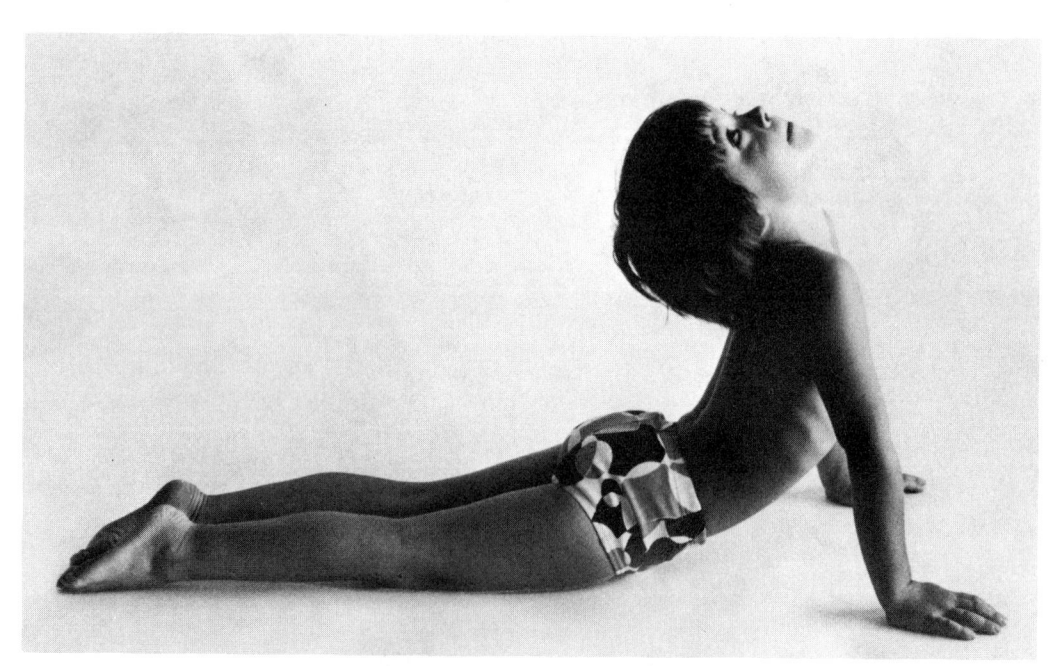

LOOK UP *Raise the torso so neck is arched and elbows are straightened.*

RHYTHMIC MOVEMENTS FOR AGILITY, BALANCE, AND CONTROL

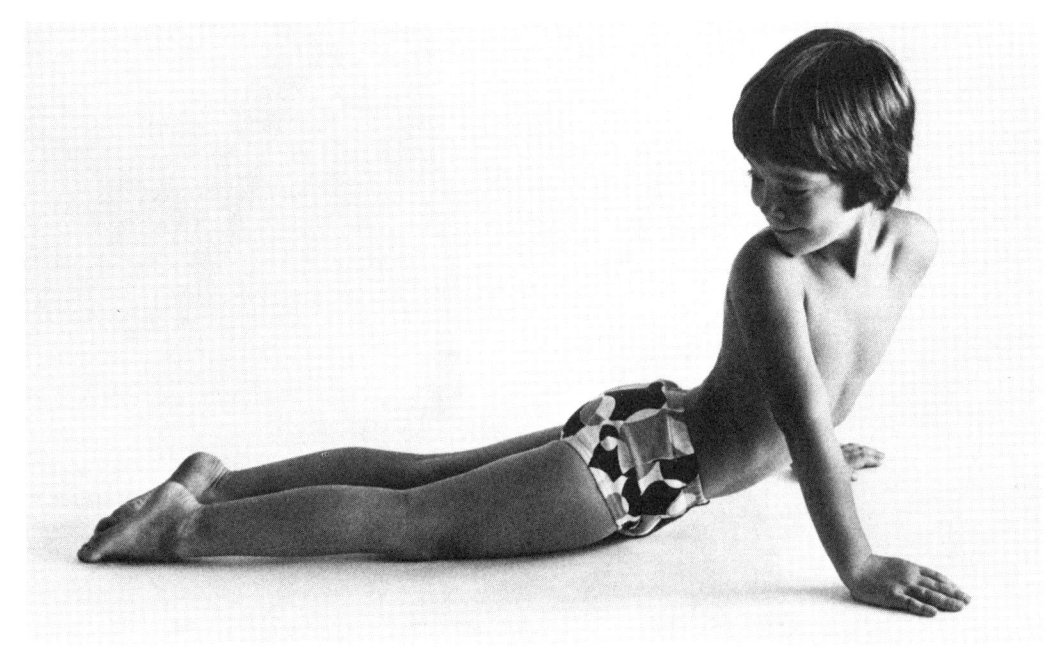

TURN AROUND *While arms are stretched and legs together, turn the head to look over the right shoulder, then over the left shoulder.*

RHYTHMIC MOVEMENTS FOR AGILITY, BALANCE, AND CONTROL

CUT WOOD LIKE A WOODCHOPPER These rapid, vigorous movements release pent-up energy, and are especially appealing to hyperactive children. Control is developed in manipulating different parts of the body by bending, stretching, and pulling with force. The woodchopper makes a good counting game for three-year-olds.

Stand with feet apart. Interlock fingers and stretch arms up over the head, bending the spine. Tense muscles to feel force of movements. Swing imaginary axe down while bending the spine forward. Continue movements to develop a smooth body swing. Practice deep breathing. Inhale while stretching upward, exhale while forcefully bending down.

RHYTHMIC MOVEMENTS FOR AGILITY, BALANCE, AND CONTROL

ROCK LIKE A SWIMMER Abdominal muscles and limbs are strengthened by the stretching up-and-down movements. Introduce deep breathing. Lie face-down. Stretch arms and legs. Inhale while rocking upward, exhale while rocking downward. Keep arms and legs taut to feel force in the movements.

WALK LIKE A MONKEY Children enjoy walking loose-limbed, letting go of their muscles. Three-year-olds will screech like monkeys if they are encouraged to combine sounds with movements.

RHYTHMIC MOVEMENTS FOR AGILITY, BALANCE, AND CONTROL

WADDLE LIKE A DUCK Bend knees with arms straight in front. Balance on toes and waddle like a duck.

(Older children enjoy these movements in a duck race.)

ROW A BOAT Sit with legs together. Make fists and stretch arms out. Use abdominal muscles to pull up and down as if rowing.

52 RHYTHMIC MOVEMENTS FOR AGILITY, BALANCE, AND CONTROL

RIDE A BICYCLE Lie on back, arms to the sides, palms down. Raise legs, and move them as if peddling the wheels of a bicycle.

Turn this exercise into a counting game for three-year-olds.

When abdominal and back muscles are strengthened, raise legs above the head. Securely bracing the elbows, support waist with arms. Then rotate legs.

RHYTHMIC MOVEMENTS FOR AGILITY, BALANCE, AND CONTROL

CRAWL LIKE A TORTOISE Limber children who have a wide range of flexibility can crawl like a tortoise by pressing down on the palms to move forward. Tight-muscled children should practice the forward stretches in gradual stages. This three-year-old is helped by his sister, who coaxes him gently. "Just a little further," she tells him, "and you'll be a tortoise."

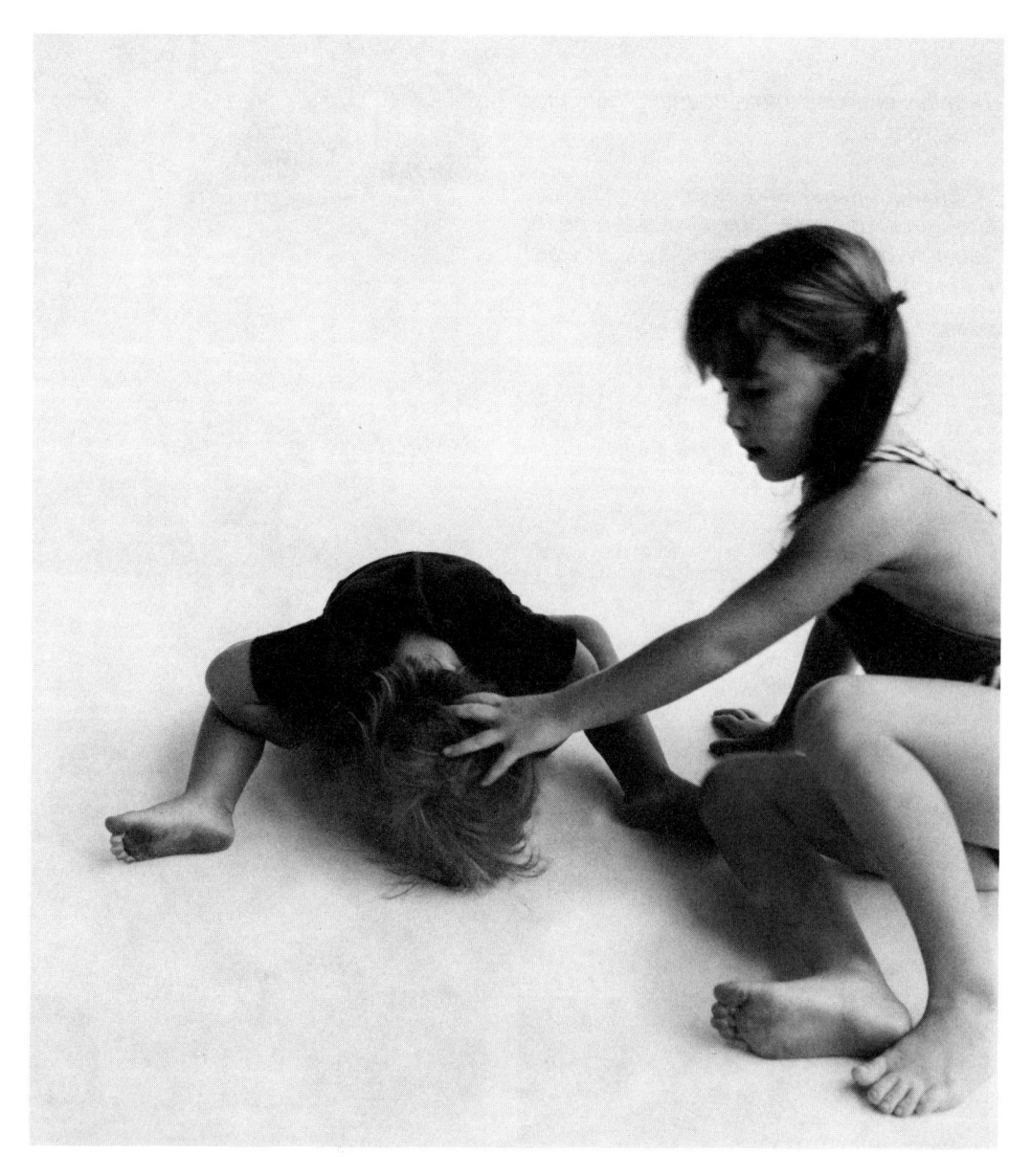

Sit with legs outstretched, far apart. Hold the ankles.

Bend forward, stretching slowly until the head is down.

When muscles have limbered sufficiently, slip arms under the legs, palms down.

RHYTHMIC MOVEMENTS FOR AGILITY, BALANCE, AND CONTROL

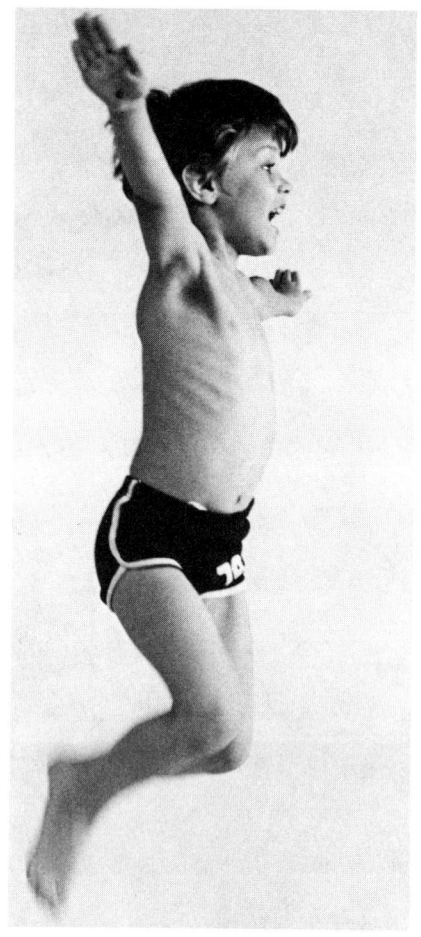

KICK *Stand straight. Kick the left leg as high as possible, with arms stretched out. Repeat with the right leg. With each kick try to get the leg a little higher.*

JUMP *Stand straight. Jump as high as possible with arms stretched out. When touching the ground each time, jump a little higher and faster.*

RHYTHMIC MOVEMENTS FOR AGILITY, BALANCE, AND CONTROL

BE A JACK-IN-THE-BOX Squat on toes with arms straight in front. Jump up and down.

RHYTHMIC MOVEMENTS FOR AGILITY, BALANCE, AND CONTROL

BE A JUMPING JACK Stand with legs apart and arms outstretched to the sides. Jump and clap hands over the head. Repeat movements rapidly.

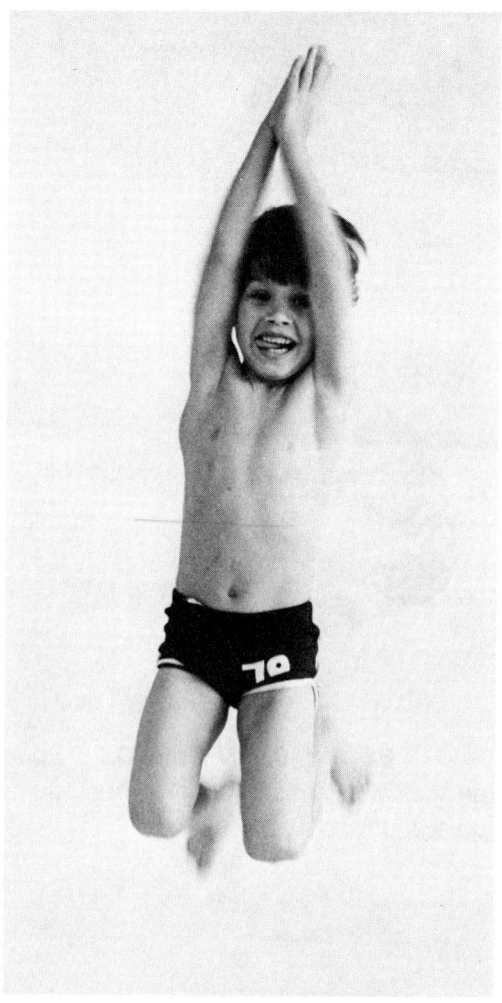

RHYTHMIC MOVEMENTS FOR AGILITY, BALANCE, AND CONTROL

TURN A SOMERSAULT *Bend with head touching the mat, knees tucked under the body. Press down on the palms and roll over. Repeat several times without stopping, to develop agility and fluid movement.*

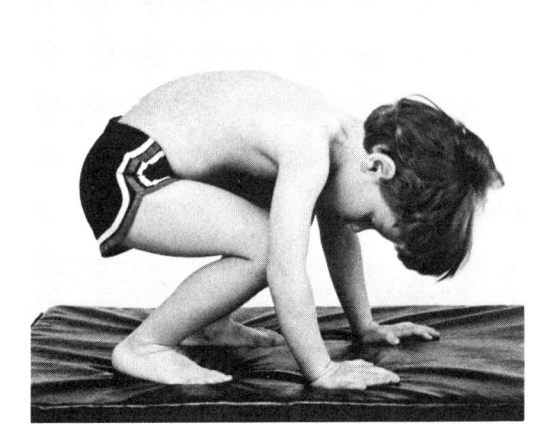

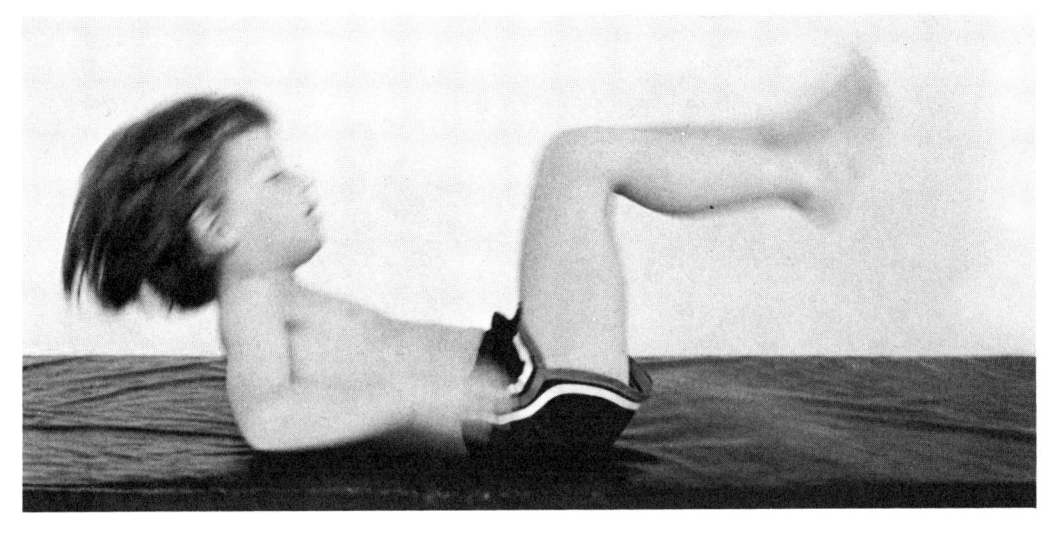

RHYTHMIC MOVEMENTS FOR AGILITY, BALANCE, AND CONTROL

BE A ROCKING HORSE Sit with knees close to the body. With fingers interlocked, wrap arms around the legs. Without letting go of hands, rock back and forth, keeping head close to knees.

60 　　RHYTHMIC MOVEMENTS FOR AGILITY, BALANCE, AND CONTROL

FUN WITH A PARTNER

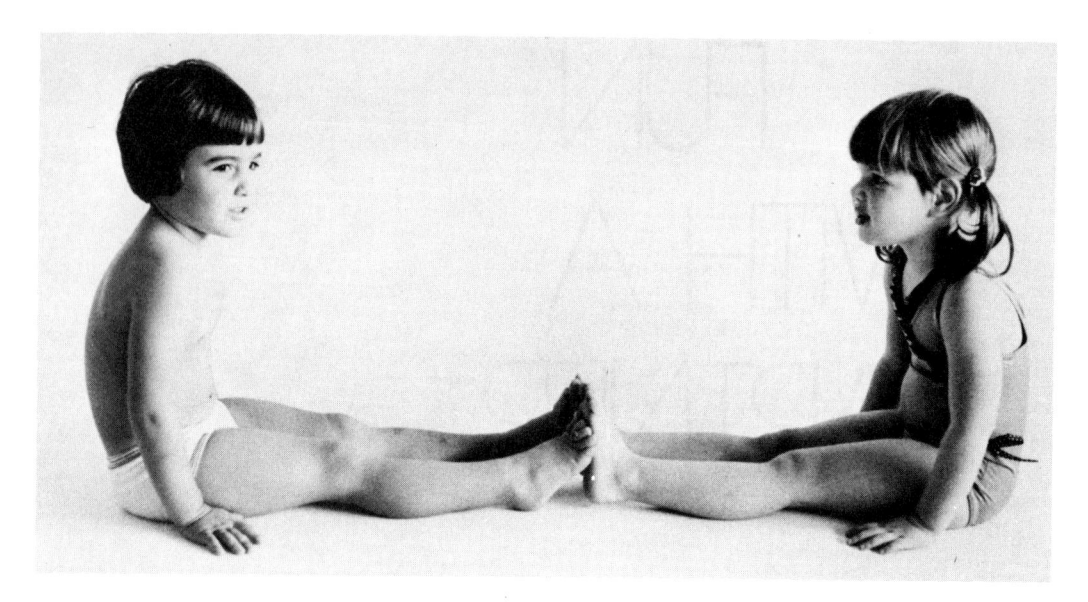

SITTING LETTER "U" *Partners sit opposite each other with soles of feet touching. Exercise feet by pushing the soles against each other.*

LYING LETTER "U" *Partners lie opposite each other, heads touching, arms to sides, and legs raised straight up.*

FUN WITH A PARTNER

LETTER "W" Partners sit opposite each other with feet touching, knees bent. To raise legs, press down on palms with soles of feet touching. When counterbalance is secure, legs can then be straightened.

FUN WITH A PARTNER

SEE-SAW *Sit opposite each other. Legs apart, soles of feet touching. Hold hands tightly with arms fully stretched. Keep backs straight. One partner leans back to pull the other forward. Each uses restraint. When one pulls back, the other pulls forward. Movement is continuous.*

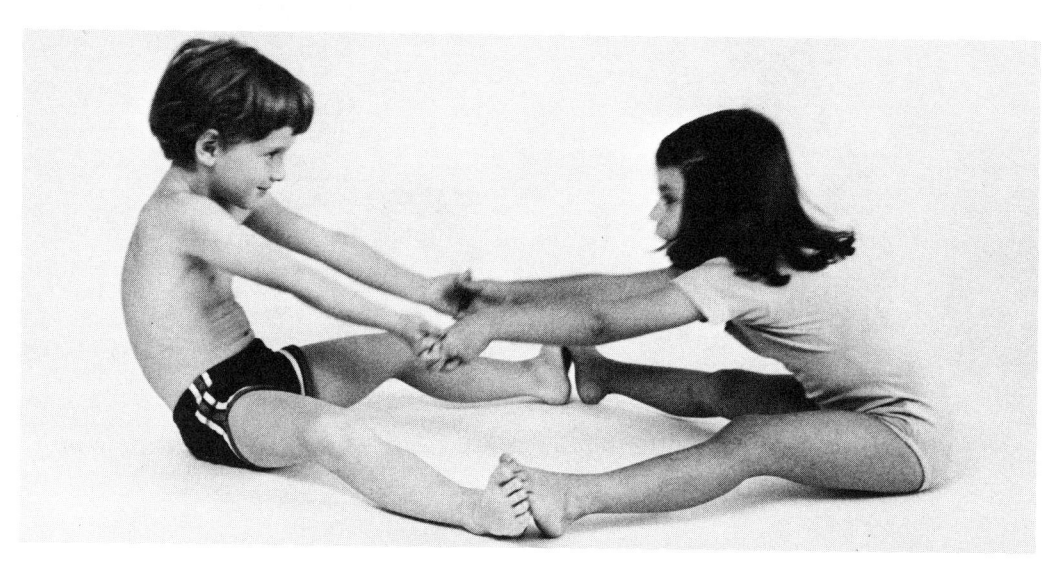

TOES MEET *Lie flat opposite each other, heads touching. Stretch arms and hold hands. Raise legs over the head to meet toes of partner. Hold with toes touching, then lower legs. Turn this into a counting game in which movement is continuous.*

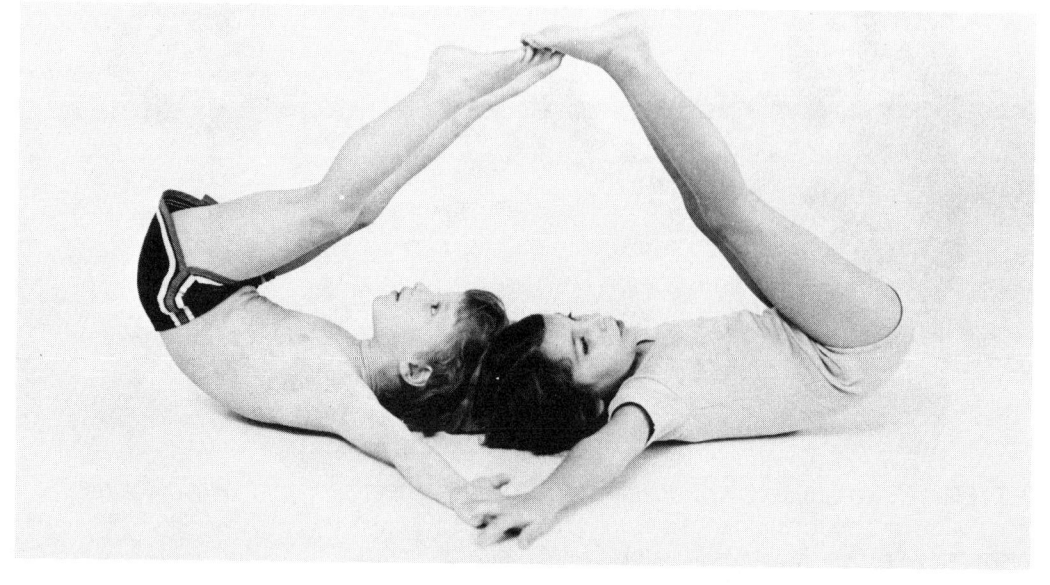

FUN WITH A PARTNER

STRETCH AND BEND *Face each other, feet touching. Hold hands. When one partner squats, the other pulls back, using force for better balance. Without letting go, each partner takes a turn squatting and standing, in an up-and-down movement.*

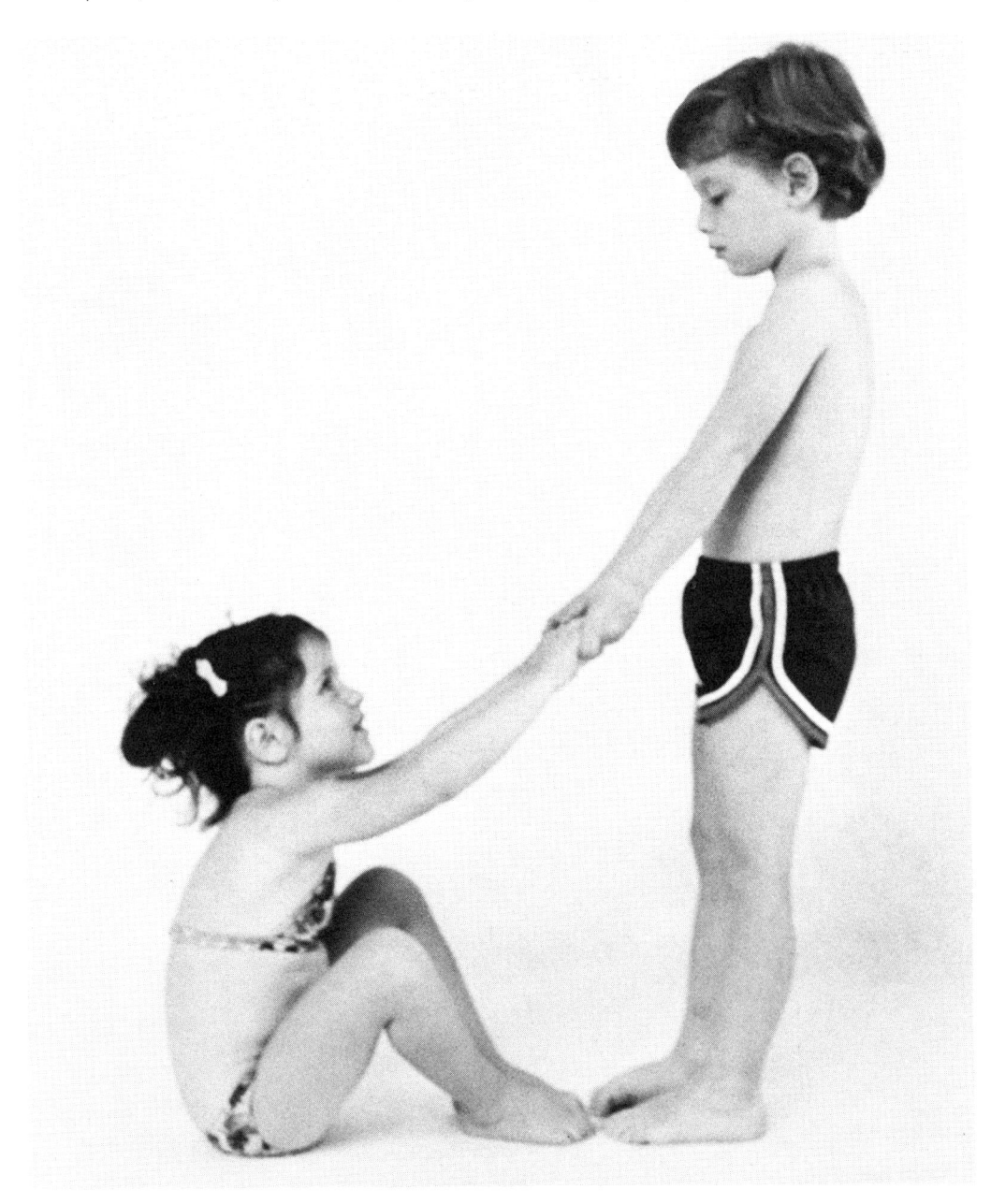

FUN WITH A PARTNER

PULL A WHEELBARROW *Walk on hands while one partner holds onto the ankles of the other and pushes forward. This can be turned into a wheelbarrow race.*

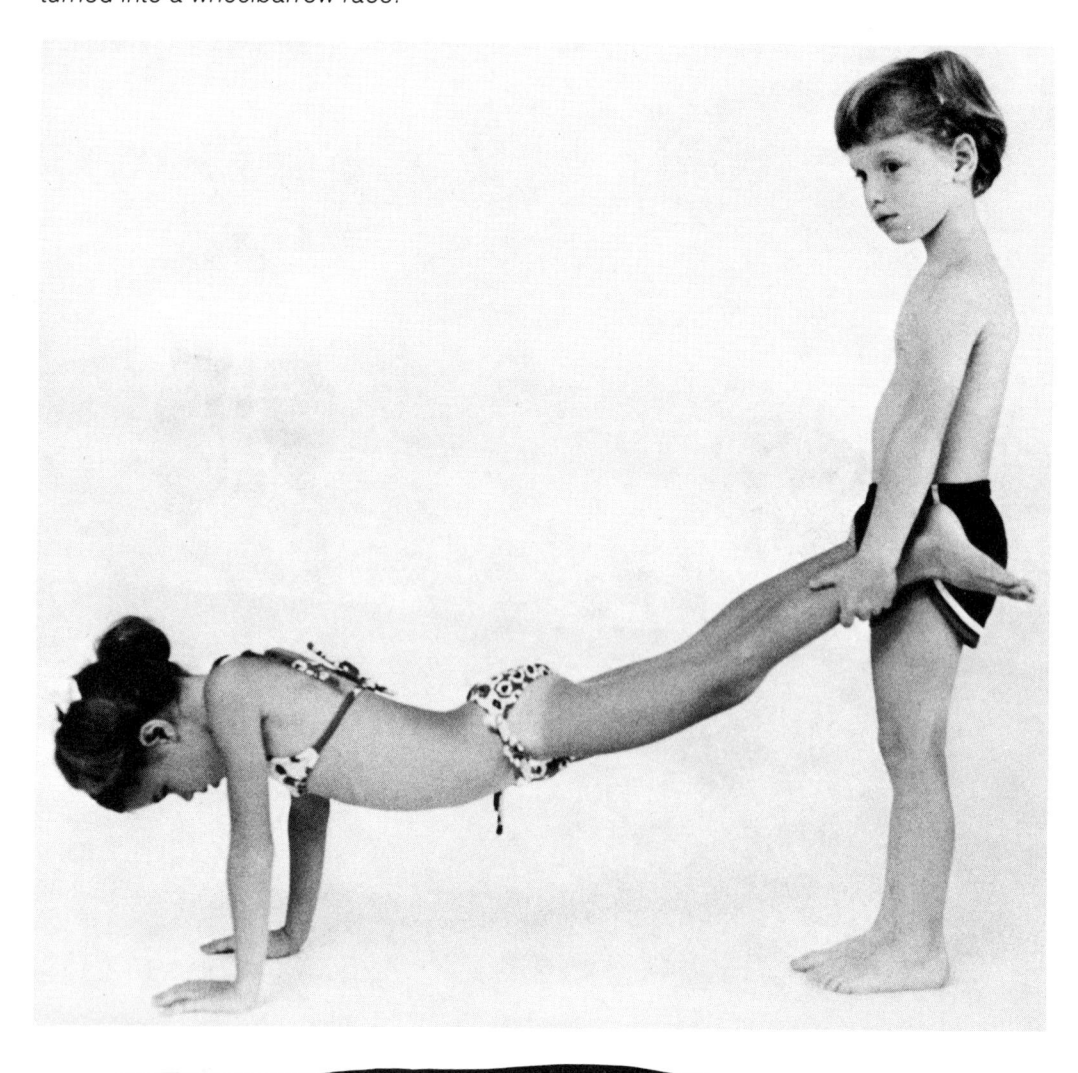

FUN WITH A PARTNER

GAMES CHILDREN LIKE TO PLAY

BODY GAMES FOR THREE-YEAR-OLDS

1. How tall can you be?
2. How small can you be?
3. How round can you be?
4. How wide can you be?
5. How thin can you be?
6. How high can you jump?
7. How happy can you look?
8. How sad can you look?
9. How angry can you look?
10. How tightly can you close your eyes?
11. How wide can you open your eyes?
12. How wide can you open your mouth?
13. How far can you stick out your tongue?
14. How tightly can you squeeze yourself?
15. Can you balance on tiptoes?
16. Can you hop on one leg?
17. Can you balance on one leg?
18. Can you bend and touch your toes?
19. Can you roll your head in a circle?
20. Can you twist your body to the right, then to the left?
21. Can you be the letter "L"?
22. Can you be a mountain?
23. Can you fly like a bird?
24. Can you prowl like a lion?
25. Can you ride a bicycle?
26. Can you be a windmill?
27. Can you hop like a frog?
28. Can you zoom like an airplane?
29. Can you swim like a fish?
30. Can you walk like a monkey?

BODY GAMES FOR FOUR- AND FIVE-YEAR-OLDS

1. Balance on your toes and reach for the sky.
2. Bend down and touch the ground.
3. Close your eyes and see the darkness.
4. Open your eyes and see the brightness.
5. Listen with your ears and hear sounds.
6. Close your ears and shut out the sounds.
7. Take a deep breath and fill your lungs with air.
8. Let out your breath to empty your lungs.
9. Spread your fingers and make them stiff.
10. Bend your fingers and make a fist.
11. Kick one leg as high as your head.
12. Wrap your arms around your body to feel your warmth.
13. Can you be the letter "V"?

14. Can you be the "flying letter V"?
15. Can you bend like a camel?
16. Can you float like a fish?
17. Can you balance like a stork?
18. Can you sleep like a hare?
19. Can you stand like a tree?
20. Can you be a strong slide?
21. Can you ride a bicycle?
22. Can you row a boat?
23. Can you slither like a cobra?
24. Can you cut wood like a woodchopper?
25. Can you be a rocking horse?
26. Can you hop like a frog?
27. Can you be a jumping jack?
28. Can you be a jack-in-the-box?
29. Can you waddle like a duck?
30. Can you turn a somersault?

GUESSING GAMES IN PANTOMIME

Have children sit in a wide circle. Select one child at a time to enter the center and perform a body shape for the others to guess. It can be an image of an animal, bird, or object that they have learned. Great excitement builds up in this type of pantomime, as each child enters the circle eager to become the center of attention.

Apart from providing personal enjoyment, this game helps children develop a more retentive memory and capacity for recalling body images they have learned.

RACES AND CONTESTS

The vigorous movements of a jumping frog, somersault, waddling duck, and wheelbarrow make exciting races. To avoid confusion, select about four children at one time.

The jumping jack and jack-in-the-box exercises can be turned into a contest of counting the number of times a child can repeat the same movements without stopping.

The different shapes of a tree, flying letter "V", and stork are a lot of fun in a balancing contest.

These are only some ideas of what can be done with the different exercises in the book.

THE WORLD OF IMAGERY

see and be
is a game of fun.
you'll be many things
one by one by one.

there go the birds
way up high
follow them up—
fly! fly! fly!

THE WORLD OF IMAGERY

birds ride the wind
like boats ride the sea.
stretch your arms back
and a bird you'll be.

THE WORLD OF IMAGERY

THE WORLD OF IMAGERY

THE WORLD OF IMAGERY

can you be a woodchopper?
a chopper of wood?
just give it a try,
i know you'll be good.

lift up your axe,
swing it up high,
then bring it down quickly—
make the chips fly.

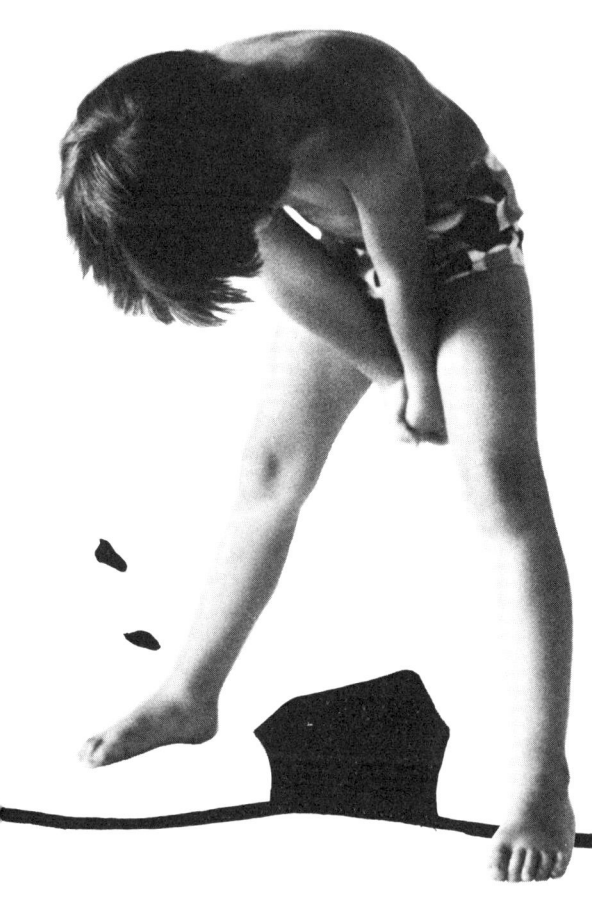

THE WORLD OF IMAGERY

frogs hop about
the whole day long.
they never get tired,
their legs are strong.

THE WORLD OF IMAGERY

to hop like a frog
you bend down low.
put your hands on your head
and push with your toes.

THE WORLD OF IMAGERY

when a cobra slithers
upon the ground,
it raises its head
to look around.

THE WORLD OF IMAGERY

it sometimes makes
such hissing sounds
that people run off
in leaps and bounds.

THE WORLD OF IMAGERY

sometimes a cat is
a fat, furry ball,
other times it is
not fat at all.

arch your back up,
let it sink low,
lift up your leg,
look at your toe.

THE WORLD OF IMAGERY

you've copied the cat,
you were fat
you were thin.
i hope you did not
fall on your chin.

THE WORLD OF IMAGERY

storks are tall birds
that like to be quiet.
they sleep on one leg—
why don't you try it?

balance on one leg
with the other bent back,
put your hands together—
now how about that?

THE WORLD OF IMAGERY

when a camel kneels down
he folds his legs up
and stretches his neck
way out front.

when you kneel like a camel
don't fall in a lump.
you're not made like a camel—
you don't have a hump.

arch your back out,
put your hands on your heels,
let your head swing back—
that's how a camel feels.

THE WORLD OF IMAGERY

if you close your eyes
you will feel like a fish,
hear the water go past
with a ripple and swish.

arch your chest high
hands under your back.
it won't take you long
to get the knack.

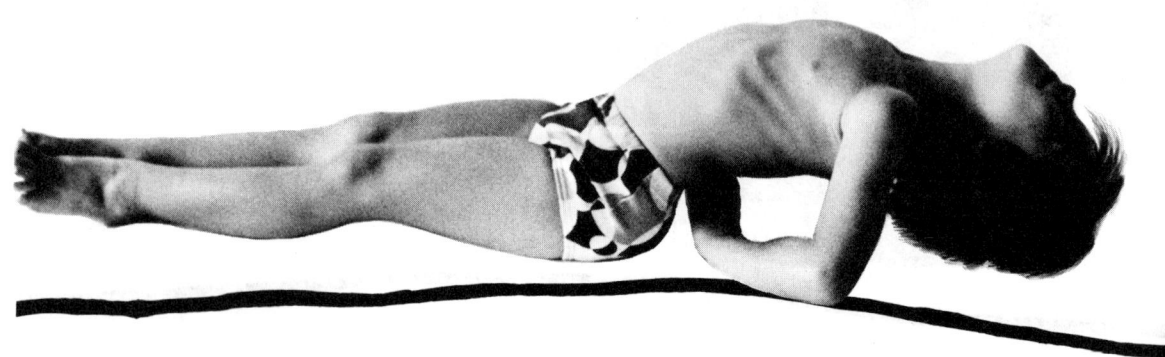

THE WORLD OF IMAGERY

put your hands together
to make the fin
that will steer you around
and back again.

THE WORLD OF IMAGERY

to be a good swimmer
stretch and stretch more,
with arms, legs, and head
up off the floor.

if you practice like this
every day
the next time you swim
people will say:

look at that swimmer
so limber and strong,
skimming the water,
racing along.

swans glide smoothly
over the water,
their proud necks
arching high,

with tail feathers
ruffling in the wind.
look at them
sailing by.

bend your legs
to touch your head,
you are no longer you,
you're a swan instead.

THE WORLD OF IMAGERY

some mountains are high,
some mountains are low.
stretch yourself up,
see how high
you can go.

THE WORLD OF IMAGERY

to make your own mountain
there's a thing you should know,
start at the bottom
with your legs crossed, just so.

then lift your arms up to the sky
so your hands make the very high
peak.
you can play a game
with fluffy white clouds,
a game of hide-and-seek.

the tips of your fingers
are the top of the tree
which waves in the wind
so easy and free.

THE WORLD OF IMAGERY

one leg is the trunk
with its roots so long,
the other is bent—
it's not straight,
but it's strong.

THE WORLD OF IMAGERY

THE WORLD OF IMAGERY

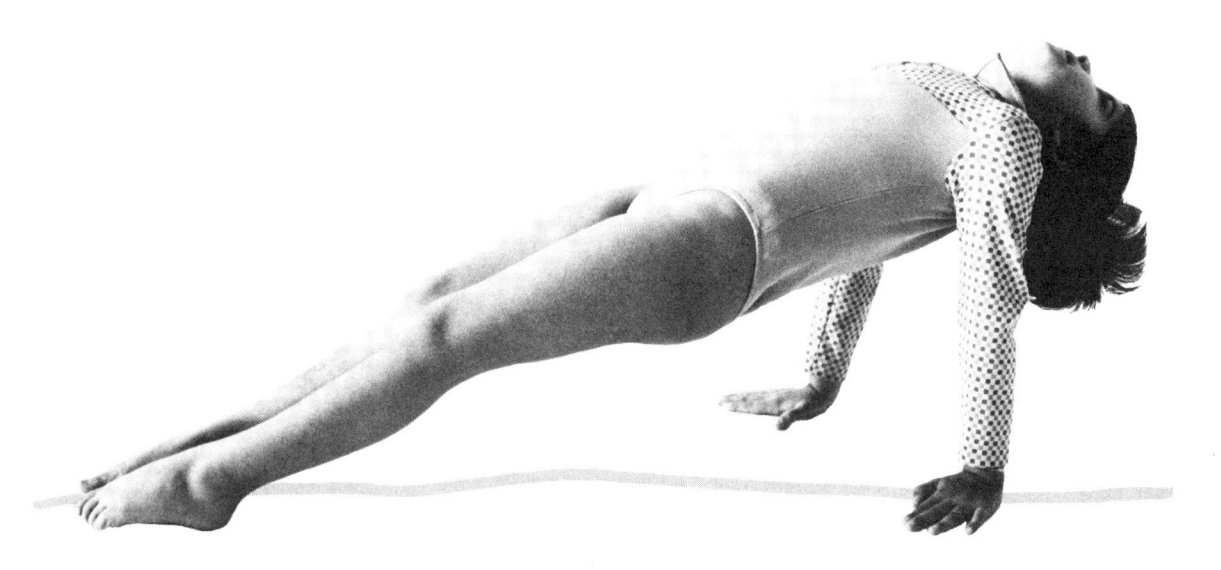

you are the slide
in the park
where you go to play
with a friend.

stretch your legs out,
keep your back very straight.
make sure the slide
does not bend.

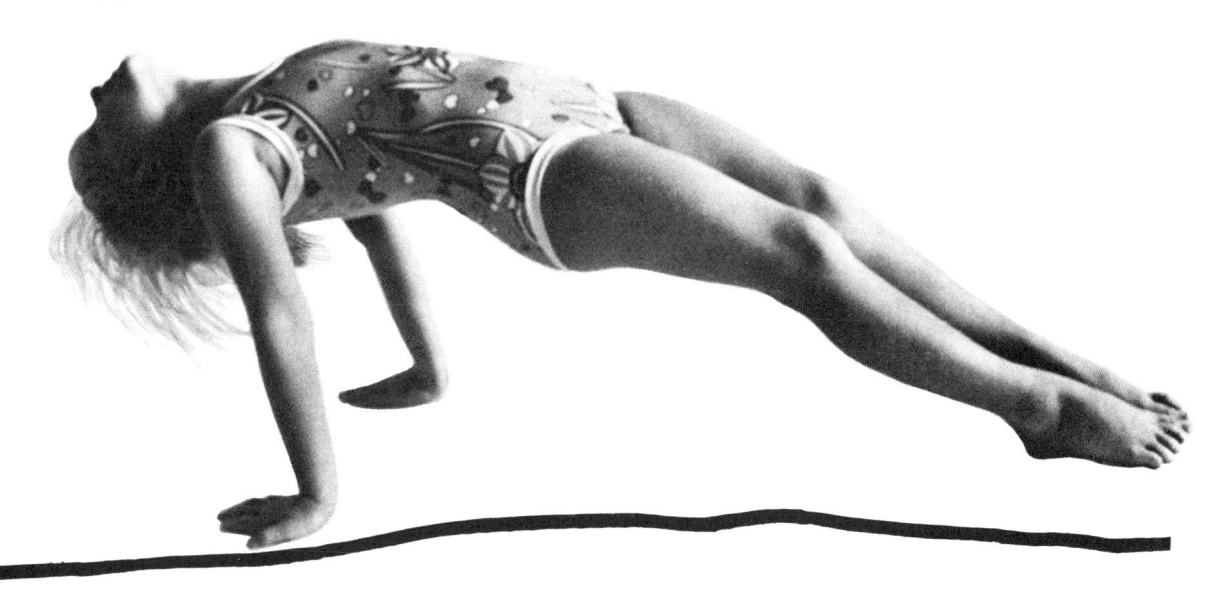

THE WORLD OF IMAGERY

right from the start
you can certainly tell
the tortoise will lose
with that big, heavy shell.

you are a tortoise,
your friend is a hare.
you are starting a race
that does not seem fair.

THE WORLD OF IMAGERY

with hands under your legs
a tortoise you will be.
now bend your head down
to make the shell, you see.

the sun is hot,
the hare stops by a tree
to take a short nap,
his head near his knee.

THE WORLD OF IMAGERY

look what has happened!
can I believe my eyes?
the tortoise has won it—
has won the first prize!

z z z z z

THE WORLD OF IMAGERY

when you sit straight
it is easy to tell
that the letter you make
is the one called "L".

this is another
for your friend and you,
with heads together,
you make a "U".

THE WORLD OF IMAGERY

your legs and your back
make the letter "V".
stretch out your arms
and it flies, you see.

you and your friend
with feet in front of you
put two "Vs" together
and now it's a "W".

THE WORLD OF IMAGERY

the day is ended,
the flying is done,
home come the birds,
one by one.

THE WORLD OF IMAGERY

they sit on a tree
all together.
they stretch and they yawn
and they flutter their feathers.

then they tuck their heads
under their wings
and dream little bird dreams
of wonderful things.

ASSESSMENT OF PROGRESS CHARTS

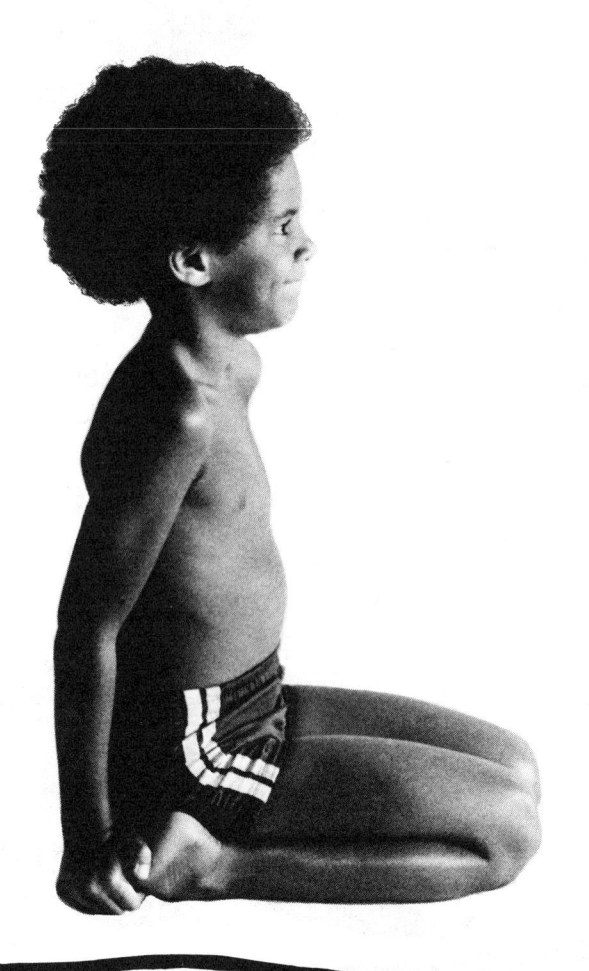

ASSESSMENT OF PROGRESS

CHILD'S NAME AND AGE	PROBLEM	PROGRESS

ASSESSMENT OF PROGRESS

CHILD'S NAME AND AGE	PROBLEM	PROGRESS

ASSESSMENT OF PROGRESS

CHILD'S NAME AND AGE	PROBLEM	PROGRESS

ASSESSMENT OF PROGRESS

*CHILD'S NAME
AND AGE*   *PROBLEM*   *PROGRESS*

ASSESSMENT OF PROGRESS

CHILD'S NAME AND AGE	PROBLEM	PROGRESS

ASSESSMENT OF PROGRESS

CHILD'S NAME
AND AGE *PROBLEM* *PROGRESS*

ASSESSMENT OF PROGRESS CHARTS